Dear Ste

Ecc 5:10

Blessings always,

Gabriele Rie—

Own It
Stepping up to Intentional Living

Gabriele Rienas, MA, LPC

For Werner, my teenage sweetheart,
who has grown with me
and has constantly provided reasons to laugh
every step of the way.

CONTENTS

Author's Note

My worldview is faith based. I believe that God exists, that he intentionally and uniquely created me and passionately loves me. I believe there is a divine plan for my life that fits like a puzzle piece into God's entire divine plan for the planet. I believe his love is unconditional, not coercive but invitational, not apathetic but encouraging, not demanding but lavish. He invites me into a relationship with him in which we together walk out the circumstances of my life. He loves me unconditionally yet invites me to become more fully myself, learning and growing every day with his help and grace. In the process he more adequately fulfills his will through me.

After looking at the way things are on this earth,
here's what I've decided is the best way to live:
Take care of yourself, have a good time,
and make the most of whatever job you have
for as long as God gives you life.
And that's about it.
Ecclesiastes 5:18

INTRODUCTION

Do you mind if I just sit this one out?

Squirming uneasily in my seat, I pushed away the rogue thought and tried to look inspired as the motivational speaker urged us to abandon ourselves to the pursuit of a more fulfilling life. She humorously and eloquently implored us to press past our self-inflicted limitations into maximum living. She reminded us that God has given us all special gifts and talents that we are to embrace and capitalize upon for greater impact on our personal sphere of influence. The possibilities of what we could accomplish were limitless if we put our whole hearts into it. As I glanced around the crowded room, it seemed that everyone else was totally moved, ready to leap up out of his or her seat and hurry home to start changing the world. I, on the other hand, felt vaguely detached...and well...tired.

It wasn't that I didn't want to make an impact on my

world; I had spent a great deal of time and energy pursuing that goal. I did—and still do—crave to know that I matter and that my life makes a difference on the planet. In fact, as a faith-based motivational speaker, I publically had encouraged people to pursue that very thing many times. However, that night, the idea of watching from the sidelines as everyone else scurried about greatly appealed to me. I felt a bit like a young child who sits in the middle of the street and refuses to walk any farther despite her parents' efforts to coax her onto her feet. Arms crossed, I was done. Of course the idea was immediately followed by feelings of guilt about my inner resistance to pursuing greatness. Apparently much would be left undone if I failed to show up with my unique contribution to the world.

In defense of the speaker's exhortation that night, I must admit that everyone wants to live a life that makes a difference. Meaningless existence is not an option for members of the human race. If we fail to make a positive contribution, we become part of the problem. Looking back on that evening, however, I realize my thoughts reflected an emerging dilemma. *How do we find authentic meaning without exhausting and discouraging ourselves in the pursuit of it?*

The answer starts deep within us. It has very much to do with making peace with the person we are and what life has brought our way. This inner foundation then becomes the starting place from which we launch into the world. I fear that in some instances we have launched without first taking care of our own business. We cannot fully give ourselves until we own who we are, what we have gone through, and what might hinder us from moving forward.

We are all humans in the process of becoming. We are individual blends of strength and weakness, personality, experience, and passion. We each choose whether we are destined to stay stuck in one place forever or whether we'll allow all of those pieces to be refined bit by bit as we walk out our lives.

Let me give you an example of such a refining moment in my life. My friends urged me to share this story, but I have mixed feelings about it. On the one hand, I love to laugh, and the story is rather funny. On the other hand, it's embarrassing. I always emphasize that it happened many years ago. I remember the approximate date because my niece was a baby in a car seat at the time, and she's now grown up.

My sister was visiting with my niece from out of town. We were driving around town when I decided that my car needed to be washed. Our neighborhood carwash has an unusual entrance. There are two options when you pull off the street. Either you make an awkward U-turn to get into the line of cars, or you drive around several buildings and maneuver into line with a bit more finesse.

That particular day it seemed half the city wanted a carwash. The endless line of cars snaked around several buildings. I decided the U-turn option was more convenient for me. Since I'm a rule follower (sort of), cutting into line wasn't an option, so I made a mental note of my place in the lineup. I noted a navy-blue van—the last car in the line coming toward me—and decided I'd slip in after it passed me. This made perfect sense to me. I waited patiently, moving forward only after the targeted van passed. Unfortunately the drivers of the cars that had now filed in behind the van knew nothing of my immaculate reasoning and simply thought I was cutting into the line. Immediately behind the van was a black Eldorado with a young man behind the wheel. Surprisingly he didn't look upon my efforts to inch into line with kindness. His hostile eyes met mine through the windshield, and in that instant something triggered in my brain. I decided I was going to win this battle by edging my vehicle ahead of his, because I was right. With hand gestures I indicated that it was my turn and that I was next in line. Using a few hand gestures of his own, he let me know that he didn't agree.

Forgetting that my sister and baby niece were in the backseat, my mind focused on my need to win at all costs. As both of us inched our vehicles forward, I became prepared to sacrifice my car (not to mention my sister and my niece). In my concentration to inch past his front bumper, my car nudged the navy-blue van in front of us. It was only a small nudge—at least my mind barely registered it. Far from deterring me, it only intensified my focus. Again I inched forward, and for the second time, I nudged the van in front of me. It was the last straw. The van driver jumped out of his vehicle, followed by the Eldorado driver and myself.

We stood near the entrance of the carwash, in sight of the swirling brushes, all yelling at once, as employees ran over in an attempt to dissipate the beginning of World War III. When it was over (I did go through the carwash, and they didn't even charge me!), it was like I was coming out of a coma. I became aware of my sister sitting quietly in the backseat and suddenly wondered how she perceived what she had witnessed. Lamely I stammered an excuse and an apology. She was kind. Upon hearing the story, my husband wasn't so accommodating. He was absolutely right; I had lost my cool, and in the process, I had jeopardized my credibility and reputation. I had become a crazy person for a few minutes that day.

It's an example of raw Gabriele. That's why the story is somewhat embarrassing and why I didn't tell it for a long time. However, there is freedom in my telling the story, as the incident was one step in the process of my becoming the person I am and continue to become. In a lifetime of experiences, it was a brief moment that reflected the tension between what I wanted to appear as and who I really was. It was a teachable moment regarding expression of anger, assertion, and self-control. It was an opportunity—if I chose to make the most of it—to learn something about my vulnerabilities and myself.

I gained valuable insight when I took a good look at myself and asked myself some compelling questions about my unique contribution to the situation—in other words, when I owned it. *Owning it* means:

- Looking at "what happens to us" by factoring in who we are, where we've come from, and where we want to go.
- Taking responsibility for our contribution to every life situation.
- Asking ourselves how we have influenced the outcome of our circumstances.
- Resisting the urge to blame, deny, and rationalize our own behaviors and instead seeking to learn from self-reflection.

Only by owning it do we become empowered to spur change and choose a different path, ultimately becoming freer to pursue growth and significance. Growth and freedom come from abandoning victimization for proactive, intentional living.

Of course I had the choice to reject the whole memory and blame it on the other crazy drivers, or I could have forgotten the whole thing and never thought or spoken of it again. If I'd done either I sadly would have missed out on an opportunity to benefit from owning who I am and who I was in the process of becoming.

I might have chosen the latter options for the following reason—every person deals with two competing forces:

1. The desire to matter and make a difference in the world.
2. The desire for comfort and freedom from pain.

Unfortunately the two easily can cancel each other out. While everyone wants to make a difference, the comfort-seeking piece easily could compel us to avoid, blame, and deny those things that would bring the most peace to our souls in the long run. This book is about balancing this tension, thereby maximizing each day and living life smarter.

This is not a book about making a greater effort to become *something*. It is more about becoming *someone*. This book is about owning your life's story and extracting what you can from it in order to reach toward that maximum living everyone's talking about.

Introduction

1 GROW UP

Becoming an Adult

Recently I lamented to my husband that my profession requires me to spend my days telling people what they don't want to hear. Momentarily distracted from watching a hockey game, he remarked in his typical dry manner, "Join the club." He's a minister, and I'm a counselor, and he was right. We both face this challenge—in our personal lives and with the people we try to help. In matters that deal with the soul and with the psyche, humanity is masterful at seeing things in a way that brings maximum comfort and minimum pain. The supreme irony is that personal growth requires breaking through this natural resistance barrier and viewing the self truthfully while facing what lies within. It's the only way growth can occur. Unfortunately true growth is painful and therefore often distasteful, and so the battle is waged.

I don't often tell people to grow up. It's an "in your face," aggressive admonition, and no one responds well to hearing it. Unless pressed, I usually avoid saying it, other than occasionally to myself. But recently I said it several times in one conversation. I was speaking with a young couple, Todd and Shawna. They had been married about a year, and Todd had a six-year-old daughter, Eva, from a previous marriage. Shawna was vocal about her dislike for Eva; in fact she openly resented her very existence. When reminded that she had known about Eva before committing to Todd, she said she didn't know what she was getting into, thereby justifying her disdain for the child.

Shawna felt Todd was too lenient and constantly pressured him in front of Eva to discipline her more. In the wake of all this, Eva casually mentioned to her dad that she didn't like Shawna. She said it during a rather benign, six-year-old conversation about people in her life she liked and didn't like. Upon overhearing Eva's comments, Shawna reacted swiftly and intensely. She took the words as a personal attack and responded with disdain and punishment. Understandably the comments stung, but Shawna missed an opportunity to use the revelation to invite a closer look at the relationship. She felt the child needed to be severely disciplined for disrespectful behavior, and so ensued yet another intense, angry exchange between Todd and Shawna. The future of their relationship seemed grim.

While it seemed obvious that Shawna needed to be the

"bigger person" by accepting responsibility for decisions she had made (e.g., marrying a man with a child who was still processing the divorce of her parents), she seemed blind and resistant to this possibility. In effect she was placing herself at the level of the child by competing for attention and affection; she was ready to throw the six-year-old under the bus to maintain her own sense of well-being. I kept thinking, *Oh, grow up already!*

Of course she was in no way ready to hear my admonition and chose instead to abruptly terminate the counseling process.

This is a rather extreme example, and there are plenty of people who already have demonstrated the ability to be a bigger person in a blended family situation such as this. However, in many small ways, we are all prone to this kind of resistance to responding maturely in the face of painful circumstances. If we do act this way, we are destined to go round and round with the same problems, never figuring out why things aren't working out in our lives.

This is my challenge both to you and to myself. It's time to grow up. It's time to overcome, to bounce back, to move on, and to figure it out. I fear we're dealing with an epidemic of childishness and resistance to growth-inducing truth about ourselves. Growing up requires an intentional commitment to personal growth. It takes a dogged determination to open up to the truth about oneself, which allows the roadblocks to be revealed and challenged. It takes revelation and a willingness to listen to honest feedback. Most of all it takes the ability to say, "I am willing to learn and grow. I will be open and pursue the truth of the matter to the best of my ability. The rest I will trust to a loving God who reveals what he wills when he wills for his purposes."

Think of the most mature, grounded person you know— someone you truly look up to. What is the primary characteristic that demonstrates maturity in his or her life? Let's take a look at the qualities that demonstrate maturity. Remember that the pursuit of these qualities requires a determination and willingness to face discomfort and self-resistance in order to achieve them.

A grown-up takes responsibility.

A grown-up has *chutzpah* (definition to follow).

A grown-up speaks up.

A grown-up asks.

A grown-up has boundaries.

A grown-up sees him/herself as being equal to others.

A grown-up gets over it.

A grown-up does the right thing and does it right.

Principle 1: A Grown-up Takes Responsibility

The principle of taking responsibility is the underlying basis of maturity. It's so important that I've written an entire chapter on it. We cannot begin to be grown up until we take appropriate responsibility for what happens in our lives.

The alternative is failing to take responsibility and therefore remaining powerless. It's true. If a circumstance is not my fault, I have no power. It's as simple as that. It makes me a sitting duck, so to speak. If I did not contribute to the problem in any way, shape, or form, there is virtually nothing I can do to change the outcome. I had nothing to do with it; therefore I have no control.

Only when I begin to take responsibility for my part of the problem—for choosing to be somewhere, or for choosing to respond in a certain way, or for failing to act when I could have—can I begin to feel empowered. In the future I could make a different choice, and it would influence a different outcome. It's as simple as that.

Unfortunately our human nature makes us really good at dodging responsibility. We comfort ourselves with the knowledge that we could not have acted any differently, thereby avoiding the pain of confronting our own weaknesses.

I once worked with a couple in distress, Brea and Nick. She was quite aggressive and punitive toward her husband when she didn't get her way. She threw temper tantrums and verbally attacked him in destructive, inappropriate ways. She screamed and said cruel things to him while their children cowered in the corner with their hands over their ears; she told him she regretted marrying him and that he was sadly lacking as a husband. When she calmed down, she showed great remorse and apologized profusely for her "bad behavior." Both Brea and Nick agreed that she was clearly the problem. He had taken about all he could from her.

Without being aware of it, Nick felt quite self-righteous about the fact that he had tolerated Brea's behavior for years without retaliating. His usual response to her tirades was to hold his tongue and wait for her to calm down, while inwardly he felt bullied, belittled, and disrespected. However, he was clearly angry in a passive-aggressive manner. His displeasure came across in a dismissive, "leave me alone" sort of way. He'd shut down after an episode and disengage from Brea for several days—up to a week at a time—the whole time feeling his punishing behavior was justified. He was quite the martyr. His anger toward her was palpable and felt like abandonment to her, thereby escalating her pattern.

When I pointed out that Nick was as controlling as his wife but in a passive way, he grew indignant. I suggested he had failed to take responsibility for his part in the pattern of conflict between them. True, he inwardly protested her behavior, but he had failed to stand up to his "strong" wife and had allowed her verbal aggressiveness to dominate him. He had failed to stand firm when it was necessary. To take ownership of his part of the problem, he needed to have the courage to firmly end inappropriate conversations and draw strict boundaries when necessary, which is part of being a grown-up. In that way Nick needed to become more grown up.

He didn't like my suggestions; at first he protested, but then he finally assented by saying, "I guess I'm not ready to back down from my position of being the wounded party yet." His resentment toward Brea had become his friend and provided the comforting sensation of his being the martyr.

When we insist on being the wronged one, we stay bound up and hindered from personal growth. It's true that facing ourselves can be painful and uncomfortable. We resist it with everything in us. Facing ourselves, however, must be intentional—an act of the will. It requires a commitment to self-awareness and a dogged determination to see the truth about ourselves. Facing the pain frees us and empowers us to change the circumstances of our lives.

If we are to learn from the unwelcome circumstances in our lives, we must be willing to ask the difficult question "What is my contribution to this circumstance?" The answer is not always readily available, but it will come in good time if you have a willingness to entertain it. I discuss this more fully in Chapter Four.

Principle 2: A Grown-up Has *Chutzpah* When It Is Needed.

I recently had a meeting at a small coffee shop. The shop is gaining popularity and recognition, particularly with the local

Christian community. With its fresh and funky vibe, the atmosphere is bright and earthy, appealing to the Northwest's love for nature, space, and creativity. On top of that the baristas have a knack for ingeniously finishing a latte or mocha with a decorative leaf design in the foam. I marvel at their skill. Personally I love the ambiance of the shop and frequently suggest it as a meeting place.

I have one problem with the establishment. I don't like the coffee at all. I'm an avid mocha drinker with an insatiable and snobbish love for good chocolate. Having tried valiantly to make do with the shop's choice for mocha flavoring, I continued to dislike it, finding a specific displeasure on my taste buds while drinking it—and afterward. I finally reached the conclusion that I was no longer willing to spend money for coffee that I didn't even like.

As I mentioned, I had a meeting scheduled at the shop. While I looked forward to the fellowship, I was faced with the dilemma of the distasteful beverage. It was a morning meeting, and I was going to need coffee. To add to my quandary, it happened to be "Free Pastry Day" at Starbucks. No doubt, you're beginning to guess what I did.

I left for my meeting five minutes early, stopped in at Starbucks, purchased my mocha, eagerly received my free pastry, and made my way to the shop. Starbucks items in hand, I marched inside and settled in at a table to wait for my friend. I justified my plan because I was fairly confident she would order something when she got there, but I was a few minutes early, and she was a few minutes late. With my Starbucks coffee and Starbucks pastry, I sat there for a good twenty minutes, using the free Internet service provided by the shop! That is chutzpah!

Apparently the shop manager thought so too, because he came over and pointedly asked if he could help me with something. Funny, they never had asked me that when I was drinking their coffee.

Chutzpah (pronounced "*hutspah*"; the "u" is short) is supreme self-confidence, boldness, nerve, or sometimes an obnoxious aggressiveness. (As I look back, my example leans heavily toward the latter kind.) However, *chutzpah* is an audacity that stands up at the right moment and speaks up. It steps forward and takes responsibility.

While my coffee shop solution is atypical, the idea is that we act confidently on our values and our belief systems. It is a poise that does not shrink back but at the right moment stands tall and confident—without apology.

I'm convinced that women are innately capable of having great courage and *chutzpah*. Most women with children would stand up to a grizzly bear in full-attack mode in order to protect their offspring. This simply shows that under the right circumstances, the necessary equipment to respond boldly resides within us. I am reminded of an incident with a basketball coach when my son was in junior high. The coach belittled my son for choosing to pursue his love of piano lessons in addition to participating in sports. My response was immediate and sure, with no apology. My memory of the incident is vague, but it includes the coach backing down to my verbal barrage. Although I could have approached the matter with more finesse, the coach clearly got this message from me—"If you harm my offspring, you will be dealing with *me*!"

Other than with regard to their children, most women are afraid of having too much *chutzpah*. They abhor looking brash and awkward. In the quest to appear agreeable and uncomplicated, they go along with things, failing to speak in situations even when their voice could make a difference. The result is that for the most part, women default on the side of standing up too little, rather than too much, thereby relinquishing their impact on society.

Appropriate boldness is a trait that requires practice and development. This is good news for all of us. No matter what your default mode is (too much or too little), it can be adjusted for greater impact. However, adjustments only can happen with practice. If you wait for perfect inspiration and verbal clarity, you never will take hold of the opportunity to practice *chutzpah*. In our quest to develop boldness, we certainly will make mistakes. Still we press forward. Even blunders can become the material from which to learn and build upon. Specifically we can develop the following.

- Knowing our convictions and values.
- Assessing when it is time to speak up and/or stand firm.
- Developing our finesse regarding speaking appropriately with maximum impact.

Principle 3: A Grown-up Speaks Up

A young mom bends down before her whining, inconsolable child. He is clearly unhappy and frustrated and is letting his mother know through his annoying tones and shrieks. He refuses to cooperate or calm down, and his flailing body demands attention. Having been in this place before and having learned through experience, his mom takes the time to make eye contact and say in a clear, measured voice, "Use your words." She may have to repeat it several times, but she is coaching her son to express himself clearly and appropriately, which will make it easier for them to negotiate through the problem.

Grown-ups need to be reminded of this essential communication skill. "Use your words." "Speak up." "Lay your cards on the table." For some reason, however, many people have an aversion to direct communication and clear expression of thought. How many times have you wished that someone would know intuitively what you needed because you were reluctant to verbalize it?

Those who express themselves in this way may be admired

for their audacity, but they often are put in the category of "that sort of person." Their verbalization conjures up a kind of self-assurance that may seem overbearing or obnoxious.

It's time to challenge this perception, because it doesn't make sense. Picture a world where people go around deferring to other people, hiding their opinions while trying to guess what others want. Even if we wanted to please others, we never would be quite sure whether we actually were, and we'd have to work really hard to read body language and other subtle clues. In the end we never would really get what we wanted, and we never would know whether others were getting what they wanted.

Now picture a world where people casually but honestly state their preferences when asked. Once all the cards are on the table, decisions are negotiated with full clarity regarding where everyone stands. Everyone won't always be happy about the outcome, but there will be clarity about who stands where, and both parties can address the hard issues with more clarity.

The second world makes a lot more sense and seems much less complicated. It takes mindreading out of the equation. As in the case of the mom and the toddler, it is such a relief to finally know the truth.

The ability to communicate is a God-given gift. Your voice is more than the sound that comes from your vocal chords. It is the part of you that communicates; it is your contribution, your input to the world around you. It is the part of you that intersects with the world around you and makes an impact. A grown-up uses his or her voice clearly, intentionally, and purposefully.

In any given situation, your voice is either present or absent. When you use your voice, you insert a piece of yourself into the context around you, and it makes a difference to the outcome every time (whether it is good or bad). When you fail to speak, you become absent and non-present; you fail to insert yourself into the world around you. There may be times when you choose to stay silent, but the choice should be intentional and deliberate rather than your default mode.

The following passage from Scripture makes the point well.

A wise person gets known for insight; gracious words add to one's reputation. True intelligence is a spring of fresh water, while fools sweat it out the hard way. They make a lot of sense, these wise folks; whenever they speak, their reputation increases. Gracious speech is like clover honey— good taste to the soul, quick energy for the body. (Proverbs 16:21–24)

Go ahead. Lay your cards on the table. Start a new trend in your circles and practice speaking up while at the same time acknowledging and praising others who do so.

Principle 4: A Grown-up Asks

I was at a meeting with a group of businesswomen recently. During the meeting I made a mental note to speak about a business matter with a woman who sat across the room from me. It was to her benefit that we speak, because I was going to ask her for her services. (I planned to pay her of course.) After the meeting I made my way over to my colleague, and I wasn't slow about it. Even though I took the most direct path across the room, I quickly realized that another woman already had entered into a conversation with her. I resorted to that polite—but visible—stance one takes when waiting to speak with someone who's already engaged in conversation.

She saw me out the corner of her eye, and I resolved to wait patiently until she finished her conversation. I say I "resolved," but in actuality I started out waiting patiently enough, but after about five minutes, I began to shift from one leg to another. I tried to keep my negative, impatient thoughts at bay. *No matter*, I thought. *I'll collect my coat and belongings and come back. Surely by then she'll be able to turn her attention to me.* A few moments later, I was back, only to find that two other women were waiting to speak with her, and they were edged in more closely than I'd been. I was now the third person in a lineup to speak with her. Unfortunately I left without having spoken her and felt frustrated about the whole thing.

I was a bit frustrated with my colleague, but I didn't allow myself that luxury for long. I knew my failure to speak up clearly had resulted in my failure to accomplish my goal. The truth is that grown-ups ask for what they need. Grown-ups do not assume others will just know or take care of their needs without being asked. Grown-ups do not expect the world to be intimately tuned into their unexpressed whims and fancies. I could have leaned forward and said, "I apologize for interrupting, but I'd really like to speak with you, and I need to leave. When would be a good time for us to talk?"

You might be gasping at the boldness of that approach. If you are gasping, you need to read this. I know many women who would not dream of doing something like that. Doing so would be forward and assertive and certainly not attractive. It would be uncomfortably close to the dreaded "b" behavior. The unfortunate truth is that women who directly ask for what they want are regarded as unattractive and pushy in some circles. It's time for women—and many men for that matter—to break through those barriers. It has held us back far too long.

Speaking up goes hand in hand with asking. Ask for what you want. Clearly and concretely ask. One of the biggest misconceptions about love is that both partners somehow can read minds and know instinctively what the other needs. I cannot count the number of times women have said to me, "If I have to ask my husband for XXX (insert desire), it doesn't count. If he loved me, he would just know." Rubbish! How would he know? God is the only one who knows all our thoughts and our needs. How narcissistic it is to believe that anyone else has the exact needs and desires as you do. It is not only narcissistic; it's ridiculous.

Others believe it's not polite to ask. If you're like me, you were taught that politeness dictates that we receive what we are offered with gratefulness and without making waves. Just be thankful for what you get without an expectation of anything else. Keeping silent, however, does not mean we are automatically grateful. In fact resentment can grow as our unspoken needs remain unmet.

Asking is not the same as demanding. Some people are just plain bossy. This is not what I'm talking about. These kinds of people bully their way around and demand that people listen to them. We see them in public settings—often retail settings—loudly demanding their rights. It's a turn-off to observe, and no one wants to be like that. I've met some wives who treat their husbands like that. These men must prove their love by giving in to their wives' desires and manipulations. Anything else is proof of great selfishness and "jerkishness."

I'm talking about an "ask" that doesn't contain a demand. These kind of "asks" start with softeners, such as "Would you mind…" or "Is it possible…" or "I'd find it helpful if…" These softeners imply that the answer is not dictated.

These "asks" are straightforward and matter-of-fact, implying that the answer could go either way. In my own life, I lay my cards on the table by revealing my preference while keeping in mind that the respondent is separate from me, with a separate life and different priorities. He or she could say no, and I'd be OK—inconvenienced perhaps but OK. I recognize that even though I may ask, the answer is never my last resort, my life-or-death solution.

Some people don't ask because they can't tolerate a "no." If they received a "no," they would feel discounted, unimportant, or unloved. They never risk asking, because they can't tolerate the answer. This is childish. People such as this lack confidence in their ability to overcome obstacles creatively.

If you don't learn to ask, you'll live a less fulfilled life. "You'll never know unless you ask." Even Madonna said, "A lot of people are afraid to say what they want. That's why they don't get what they want." I know—I can't believe I'm quoting Madonna, but she said it, and it's true.

Start practicing. Ask for small things. Ask in impersonal settings where the risk is low and where you can make mistakes; you certainly will make mistakes if you've never asked for much. Asking like a grown-up is a learned skill. It can be practiced and improved upon. Practice your tone of voice, your intensity, and your choice of words. Take a deep breath and go for it. The wonderful thing about learning a new skill such as this is that the results are reinforcing. When you ask for something, you might get what you want, and then you'll be delighted and empowered, even if just for a moment. It will give you a little more courage the next time an opportunity arises.

When you receive a "no," practice taking it graciously. Deal with your disappointment, and seek proactive alternatives and solutions without resorting to harsh tactics or embarrassing the other person. When you blow it, seek to learn from the experience; assess, examine, and adjust. Practice and learn.

Principle 5: A Grown-up Has Boundaries

I was speaking with a young woman named Alisha about her roommate situation, which seemed to be deteriorating. Several college girls were living in an apartment in order to share expenses and save money. Initially everyone had a really good time with the arrangement. There was plenty of fun interaction and happy times, and great memories were being made. It wasn't long, however, before issues began to arise over the treatment of one another's belongings. As a group they had established designated storage areas for each young woman's kitchen and food supplies, linens, and bath products. The agreed-upon arrangements, however, were not being followed, and Alisha was increasingly coming home to find her food missing from the fridge and her dishes (which she hadn't used) sitting unwashed in the sink. The final straw came when she discovered someone had used her razor in the shower, and her brand-new eye shadow palette had been opened and used. She was extremely frustrated and contemplated moving out.

These are clear examples of boundary violations—that is, overstepping one's rightful place and imposing on someone else's space. Both sides ended up with a challenge. The razor borrower was selfishly disregarding established limits, and Alisha had an opportunity to learn to reinforce her limits with those who weren't easily cooperative.

Establishing boundaries means defining one's limits and communicating those limits in order to function with maximum effectiveness. Sometimes it means saying no to something. Other times it means removing oneself from an unhealthy situation. It may mean putting extra barriers around what is being violated. Occasionally it may mean calling in reinforcements (law enforcement, lawyers, or moral support) to establish the limits. Ultimately it means finding a way to clearly say, "No means no."

Adults take care of things. They do not stand around and whine about the injustice of it all. They act to protect the lines that have been drawn. Once Alisha had identified the problem, it was up to her to decide what she could do to reinforce her boundaries. In the end she chose to accept the fact that occasionally her dishes were going to be used. She then spoke to her roommates about the use of her personal items and thereafter kept them in a place where they could not be easily accessed.

One area that requires the most attention is setting boundaries regarding what we will and will not do when others ask. If we're prone to over-committing, it's usually because we're reluctant to set boundaries regarding our time and energy. Usually this is the result of our trying to keep others happy. Unfortunately, when we over-commit, no one will be happy, and we'll be less effective in our own lives.

Given that we are all human and that humanness carries inherent limitations, it follows that we should be the "keeper" of those limitations. I have a limited amount of stamina, energy, courage, and resilience. If I disregard those limitations, I'll pay the price, and I'll end up being less effective. People should be responsible for defining their own capacity. If they don't they give up control of their lives.

For example if your mother-in-law places constant demands on your time and energy, and you acquiesce for the sake of avoiding conflict, you'll have less time and energy for other things in your life. Your mother-in-law becomes the keeper of your resources, and you'll have given up control to her. This isn't the best scenario for her or you. She may be displeased about your lack of compliance, but she too has a choice to behave like an adult or not. If she chooses to take the mature road, she'll get over it.

Some people allow everyone and everything in their lives to control them. People who do so are often outwardly compliant but inwardly angry and resentful about the intrusion on their lives. Usually they fail to admit that they have lost control over their own lives due to their unwillingness to define limits.

Some fear that boundary setting equals selfishness. Saying "no" seems contrary to a spirit of generosity and self-sacrifice. I challenge this kind of thinking with the simple fact that whenever we agree to something, we are saying "no" to something else. If I say yes to taking care of my neighbor's children while she goes to the doctor, I am saying "no" to whatever else I would have been doing during that period of time (cleaning my house, meeting a friend, writing a letter, getting caught up on finances, etc.). It's not about saying "yes" or "no," for we are always saying one with the other. It's about creating intentionality with our lives. If I agree to watch the neighbor's kids, it should be because I am intentional about giving the period of time to that act of friendship. It should not be because I don't know how to say "no," for if that's the case, I've just given up control of my life for that period of time to my neighbor.

Dr. Henry Cloud and Dr. John Townsend much sum up this concept in their bestselling book *Boundaries: When to Say Yes, How to Say No to Take Control of Your Life*. It's well worth reading.

Principle 6: A Grown-up Is Equal to Others

I remember lining up in grade school. We lined up a lot, and we all became quite good at it. We lined up to move around the school building, to get on the school bus, or to go through the lunch line. It wasn't a bad system; in fact it kept order and prevented chaos from breaking out. It didn't take us long to figure out that there were certain places in the line that were preferable to others. Of course the preference varied from child to child, but for the most part, being at the front of the line was a good thing, and being at the back of the line was a disappointment. The middle was, well, the middle. The idea was to get as close to the front of the line as possible. The triumphant leader could feel proud about asserting his or her primary place in the queue.

The human race is inexplicably drawn to hierarchical structures. "Top," "bottom," "back," and "front" all carry meaning, and we continually are tempted to assess our place in relation to the others. *Am I better or worse than the other person? Am I smarter or dumber? Am I more attractive or less attractive? Am I richer or poorer? Am I stronger or weaker?* We long to extract value from our conclusions.

I said that we are *inexplicably* drawn to this kind of structure, but maybe there is, in fact, an explanation. Could it be that at our very core we long so much for value and meaning that working our way up the ladder is one way of gaining comparative value? If I'm ahead of you, at least I have more value than you do, which suggests I am more than a zero.

Ironically this kind of ladder structure does not bring lasting value. Take a look at the people at the top of our cultural heap: the wealthiest, the most famous, the most powerful. Again and again we find that ultimately they are only human after all—a mixture of good and bad, strength and weakness, success and failure.

A grown-up continually grows in the understanding that, in relation to others, we are all equal at our core. We all—simultaneously—have the ability to live to our greatest potential while struggling with irreparable flaws. At first glance it seems like a brainteaser, but it's very simple. I came into this world unique and individual but with the same core value and potential for world impact as everyone else. I also struggle with equal human limitations and prevailing self-absorption as everyone else. Only by the grace of God and in cooperation with God's help can I seek to overcome my limitations and strive to reach toward the fullest potential he has destined for me.

Our desire for hierarchy assigns different values to various accomplishments. For example brilliantly making millions of dollars is considered far more valuable than the contribution made by a developmentally challenged person who cheerfully brings warmth into people's lives day after day.

God, however, does not have the same judging criteria. He

does not in any way see humankind in a hierarchical structure. All are equally loved, cared about, and intentionally created for purpose. All are designed to bring glory to God when they are using the blend of his gifts and his purpose in life.

We all have different personalities and gifts. This is because God is wonderfully creative. Compared to others, I am not the most nurturing person in the world. First of all I'm German, which should explain a lot of things; however, even among Germans, there are those who are much more nurturing than I. It's ironic for me to admit, as I'm a counselor. You'd think warmth and compassion would just ooze from me, but instead what oozes from me is more about common sense and straightforwardness.

Recently I ran into a former client when I was running errands. Not shy at all about acknowledging our relationship, she seemed very happy to see me and enthusiastically updated me on her life in the middle of a frozen yogurt shop. In fact she had just recommended me as a therapist to a friend. Referring to the way she described me to her friend, she happily commented, "I told her you weren't overly gushy, but very honest and good at getting to the heart of the matter." After the initial twinge of amusement, I reflected that it was an accurate summary of what I offer in therapy.

If there is a hierarchy of nurturers, I'm toward the middle of the pack, but that isn't the point. The point is that who I am—and what I have to offer—is as valuable as another who has a completely different mixture of gifts. We choose how we will apply the package we have received.

If you're doubtful about your equality with others, it will affect your life in a few ways.

- You'll shrink back and fail to speak up at appropriate times.
- You'll begin to experience that others treat you as inferior (because we train others how we are to be treated).
- You'll begin to question your purpose.
- You'll fail to set boundaries because you'll question the value of your way of seeing various situations.

The idea of utter equality before God isn't always easy to embrace. Too frequently I've had people look me straight in the eye, insisting they don't believe that God sees them equally with others. When pressed to explain why they feel this is the case, they don't have a clear answer. They just have a compelling, pressing feeling that they don't quite measure up. I come away from such conversations with sadness, and I marvel at the tenacity that humanity has to cling to a lie so fiercely. A seed of inferiority that is implanted at a very young age takes root and works its way into the very core of a life. Only the grace of God can root out such lies and replace them with the splendid, freeing truth that we are all completely equal in God's eyes.

If we all have the same potential for greatness, we also

have the same potential for failure and brokenness. Because of our fallen nature, we are all damaged as well.

Everyone needs a theology of failure. By that I mean everyone must have some sort of way of examining personal failure. This is because it will certainly happen. Everybody fails. I don't know any sane person who would disagree with this, but unfortunately there's often a disconnect between a belief that failure is universal and the grace we should extend ourselves when we do fail.

We often comfort ourselves with the fragile fantasy of self-competence and achievement so that we can feel good about ourselves. When we fail, we feel shame and a strong desire to hide and cover it up. It's almost inherent to our humanity. Adam and Eve tried valiantly to hide their shame from the very beginning of mankind.

Several years ago my husband and I got to know a family who had a little boy who was the cutest thing we'd ever seen. He was just one of those adorable kids—a towhead with a cute bowl haircut (which was fashionable at the time) and a raspy, lisping voice. The little guy didn't have a shy bone in his body, and he was very warm and loving—not to mention he could talk your ear off. One time our families were camping at the same park, and he came over to our site to tell us that he had fallen off his bike earlier that day. It quickly became apparent that he was greatly embellishing the story. His version of the tale included a bike ride inside his pup tent (an impossible feat) and climaxed with a major crash that resulted in major debilitating injuries that were in no way evident as he enthusiastically related his story. I listened intently and followed my "oohs" and "ahs" with, "Wow, did that really happen?" Even as his raspy voice assented, his head involuntarily swung back and forth in a firm "no" gesture. Unfortunately Mikie was too young to cleverly conceal his humanness, and his body betrayed him with the truth.

Growing up means going back to that state of innocence where we fess up to our failures and weaknesses. It is what it is. Everyone fails. Failure in itself is not so important. It is what follows that is essential!

As much as we resist it, owning up to our weaknesses is remarkably freeing. A certain freedom comes from bringing things to light and no longer keeping them hidden. Hiding one's true self is quite stressful and requires a significant amount of energy. You might compare it to holding a beach ball under water. It's difficult to control it so that it does not pop up.

I have a concern about a cultural shift regarding parenting. Today more and more many parents are determined to erase the possibility of failure from their children's lives. The phenomenon of the "Helicopter Parent" refers to parents hovering over their children in such a protective manner that it eliminates the possibility of their experiencing pain and failure. Good intentions are the motivating factor, but I fear that today's children are becoming increasingly weak.

Principle 7: A Grown-up Gets Over It

I'm a counselor and therefore well acquainted with the need to explore issues, communicate well, become self-aware, and engage in the process of growth. All of these things are necessary to emotional health and maturity. However, there are times in life when we should bypass introspection and just get over it. Not everything warrants our attention and emotional energy.

It's possible to err on the side of participating in so much self-reflection that a person becomes nauseatingly self-absorbed. It can become a kind of obsessive thinking that doesn't ever allow one to let go and move on.

Clara is prone to overanalyzing certain relationships to the point that it becomes debilitating and exhausting. One particular relationship with a friend named Mara is currently the source of constant angst in her life. Her friendship began well enough (as most relationships do) with mutual respect and shared goals. However, as with all relationships, there were some events that marred the perfect flow of the friendship. On days when Clara suspected that Mara wasn't as warm and engaging as usual, she felt hurt and responded with awkward silence, avoidance, and an angry countenance. Clara would spend the next few days thinking almost exclusively about the relationship. She spent hours ruminating over every moment, every word, and every look. It all seemed to have great significance, and she felt so helpless in repairing the situation. At first Mara made attempts to repair the tension when it occurred, but over time she became increasingly weary of taking the emotional lead, especially when it began to happen more frequently. This magnified Clara's feelings of rejection and started the entire loop once again.

There are definitely times when a relationship should be explored and issues should be discussed, but there are also plenty of times when it's necessary to get over a moment of tension or a perceived slight and move along. Not everything is intensely personal and worthy of deep examination.

This is true even in marriage. Not every issue will be resolved, and both partners do not always need to reach a consensus.

Principle 8: A Grown-up Does the Right Thing and Does It Right

Doing the right thing can be tough. It means living proactively rather than reactively. Unfortunately many people live reactively. They respond emotionally to a situation and react impulsively. We're also very good at justifying our actions and making them seem right in our own eyes. So we're tempted to respond reactively and then justify our actions. This way we can sleep at night telling ourselves we've done the best we could under the circumstances.

Stephanie had suffered a great deal in her marriage with Brandon. He was on the narcissistic side and clearly had "worn the pants" for the fifteen years they had lived together. He was quite black and white in his thinking, particularly regarding finances and the children. He doled out the finances meagerly and forced Stephanie to justify every purchase. Simple things, such as buying school supplies for the children, were difficult because Brandon questioned every notebook and pencil purchase. Stephanie felt like a child under his financial scrutiny. In addition he was stricter with the children than she was and second-guessed most of her parenting decisions, even though, with Brandon's busy work schedule, she was the primary childcare provider.

When Stephanie alone made the decision to allow her daughter to get her ears pierced, Brandon was indignant and brought it up repeatedly as an example of Stephanie's lack of respect for him and his authority in the house. To make matters worse, she felt greatly disconnected from Brandon, who worked long hours only to come home and lock himself in his home office. His stern demeanor had the effect of shutting her down, and she retreated further and further within herself, feeling frustrated and increasingly used.

Occasionally, over a period of several years, she tried to express her frustrations about how he was treating her, even suggesting counseling for their relationship. Brandon squashed the idea and denied there was a problem. Growing more and more resentful, she became increasingly cold and indifferent toward him, eventually toying with the idea of getting away from him altogether. As the idea took hold, it became more and more palpable, and a new life free from restraint, criticism, and domination beckoned.

At this moment your temptation might be to feel sorry for Stephanie, and you might have a few choice thoughts regarding Brandon's treatment of her. Who wouldn't feel resentful about being treated this way, and who wouldn't eventually distance themselves from such unpleasantness? Several justifications for Stephanie leaving Brandon come to mind.

- God wouldn't want her to be miserable.
- Brandon has broken his covenant by treating Stephanie as an inferior child.
- Brandon seems borderline emotionally abusive, and clearly God does not want his children to be abused.
- Stephanie has tried hard to go along with Brandon's narcissistic demands, but it's clear that boundaries eventually must be drawn.

When it finally became apparent to Brandon that he was in imminent danger of losing Stephanie, they landed in counseling. By this time Brandon was desperate and Stephanie detached and annoyed. Provoked out of her placid demeanor by Brandon's side of the story, she cried, "I've done everything for you. I gave you everything. I've tried as hard as I could. I don't know what else you want from me."

And there it was—the self-justification for her actions, which needed to be challenged. So far we've been looking at the situation through Stephanie's eyes, which makes her look pretty good (the victim who is doing her best) and makes Brandon look pretty bad.

Brandon, however, presented a different perspective. Stephanie had told the truth about Brandon's unhealthy contributions, but she conveniently had minimized her own. Brandon offered an entirely new perspective, which included a wife who was more closely attached to her children than her husband; who acted uncomfortable with Brandon's sexual advances and avoided his affection whenever she could; who clearly disdained him by rolling her eyes and shutting down and leaving the room at the slightest hint of disapproval; who had developed an affectionate Internet relationship with a former male friend from high school and kept it a secret from her husband; and who at this point barely spoke with him, clearly preferring to be with her friends and family at every opportunity.

Believing she had done "everything for him" allowed Stephanie to justify her anger toward Brandon and her plan to exit the relationship (physically and emotionally). However, it wasn't technically true that she had done "everything."

Right on the surface, there were several things she hadn't done yet.

She hadn't controlled her demeanor. She clearly was showing disdain toward Brandon by rolling her eyes and showing through her body language that she disliked and disrespected him.

She hadn't continued to pursue forgiveness toward Brandon.

She had stopped reaching out to him in loving ways; she was living under the same roof and caring for his basic needs without forging any emotional connection.

She never had really spoken up appropriately in the relationship; instead she chose to retreat and lick her wounds.

She never had set appropriate boundaries in the relationship; instead she gave in to keep the peace (another frequent justification for immature behavior).

When I asked Stephanie why she was still in the relationship, she said she was trying to do the right thing as far as what God expected and what her children needed. That was fine and well on the surface, except that she wasn't actually doing the right thing. She remained physically present, but her disdain, anger, and disconnection clearly were building huge walls. She actually was moving things in the opposite direction with her demeanor toward Brandon. Stephanie, however, resisted this suggestion because her mind was made up—she wanted out, and she wanted to believe she had done everything she could. Lest we judge too quickly, we must remind ourselves that this is common to human nature.

We want what we want, *and* we want to feel good about it. We're experts at making what we want seem OK; however, growing up means we recognize this tendency and challenge the deficits within ourselves.

It is a general human principle; we rarely have done "everything we can do." There is always more to explore; there is always another way to look at a situation; there is always another area in which we can challenge ourselves and adjust. The question is "Do we want to?"

Doing the right thing means doing the right thing and doing it right. If I'm going to stay in a relationship for the sake of the kids, I must do everything necessary to give that relationship a chance (as painful as it may be). If I'm going to give in and submit to someone, I must truly submit—with my actions, heart, and soul. If I'm going to serve someone else because it's the right thing to do, I must serve him or her, not only through my actions but also in my heart. In other words, I do what is right because it is right; my choices are not based on the actions or compliance of another.

One of the best examples of this is the relationship between ex-spouses when it comes to issues regarding the children. In cases in which one parent is clearly undermining the other—speaking badly of the other, using the children as a pawn, or trying to influence the children's feelings toward the other parent—the temptation often is to fight back in kind. If your ex-spouse verbally demeans you, you will at the very least be tempted to defend yourself and correct the injustice. However, this isn't in the best interest of the children. Grown-ups do what is right because it is right. Another's actions do not influence this. Treat your ex with respect because it is the right thing to do for your child. Even if he does not respond in kind, continue to do the right thing. This requires self-restraint, discipline, and maturity.

As a general rule, society is requiring less and less maturity from its members. It seems that a vast amount of resource and energy is spent focusing on appeasing the weakest among us, causing us to lose our own potential for greatness. It's almost like we no longer expect maturity from one another and thereby dilute our strength. Change comes only when individuals begin to pursue maturity and self-development, investing in the things that bring personal growth, no matter the cost.

2 BECOME AWARE

Seeing Yourself

One day when our daughter Alison was a teenager, she and I were listening to a radio talk-show psychologist as we drove home from school. The Doctor was being her usual impatient but straightforward self. This particular day the caller was doing the common "I want advice but will argue with any solution you offer because I prefer to be stuck" dance. In a fit of exasperation, the talk show guru exclaimed, *"Why* are you arguing with me? My logic is impeccable.*"* Alison and I hooted with laughter at her audacity. She brazenly voiced what mankind so often believes—that one's personal perspective is absolutely valid and right.

It's human nature to think in such a way so as to maintain a comfortable view about ourselves. We prefer to give ourselves the benefit of the doubt, to rationalize our motivations, and to justify our decisions. Think about the last time someone around you made an adamant declaration about the right way to complete a task. You probably immediately compared the idea with your own way of doing things and either felt validated if it was the same or defensive if it was different.

We must resist this self-gratifying perspective in order to learn about ourselves and therefore grow. To make life corrections, we must be willing to face the truth about ourselves, which can feel very uncomfortable. The natural tendency is to cling to the façade that we're OK. We resist and rationalize uncomfortable truths consciously and unconsciously.

I'm thinking of two situations that came up recently. The first relates to my friend, Candice, who went through a counseling course with me. As part of the class, we read books, studied, and discussed relationships, healthy living, and helping skills. We learned much about dealing with personal issues and recovery in our lives.

In the class we specifically talked about marriage and explored practical ways to help people with relational difficulties. The topic of marital affairs was explored. How does it happen? What are the devastating effects? What are the steps to successful recovery? Candice was an active participant in the class. She shared openly about her own marriage, which she repeatedly claimed was very healthy.

Over time it gradually became apparent that all was not

well in Candice's life. Something was amiss, and her marriage seemed to be taking a hit. Our classmates observed a downward emotional spiral taking place and became concerned about her. Eventually the truth emerged. Over a period of several years, she had been acting out inappropriately in a way that had undermined her marriage. Our classmates rallied around her with support and counsel, and she seemed grateful for it. We soon learned, however, that she went back and forth between repairing things with her husband and reengaging in her destructive behaviors. Her relationship with her husband became a roller coaster of highs and lows, with starts and stops as promises were made and repeatedly broken.

I was somewhat bewildered and asked myself, How did this happen? Candice clearly had participated in a learning environment that explored and examined the downfalls of this kind of behavior. We even had focused on ways to help people avoid the pitfalls and the resulting destruction. How could there have been such a great disconnect between what she had learned and the choices she was making? What rationalizations allowed her to bypass educated common sense?

The second situation involved a premarital couple that had an idealized view of their relationship. It's not uncommon for premarital couples to wear rose-colored glasses. I've come to accept this phenomenon when I work with couples before their marriage. I'm not trying to be negative about marriage, but I'm convinced that without some form of those blessed glasses, no one ever would get married.

This particular couple, however, presented some severe red flags. Both of them had some obvious unaddressed relationship dramas in their past, not to mention some glaring personality conflicts in their current relationship. On top of this, they had dated for a very short time and were rushing toward a wedding within weeks of having begun counseling. I gently tried to insert my concerns, but as often happens, the couple brushed them aside.

Then a crisis hit. They had a full-blown drama-filled fight that lasted a week. During the course of the devastating week, one or both of them experienced panic attacks, episodes of hysteria, despair for living, and periods of disassociation. These were clear indications of fairly significant deeper problems that were emerging. Eventually, however, they made up and reconnected. When the emotional windstorm blew over, the couple tried to make sense of the blowup by saying it had been some kind of mutual misunderstanding that never would happen again.

We had a heart-to-heart session after that, and I spoke with them about postponing the wedding in order to explore the root behind these kinds of interactions to make sure they knew what they were getting into. I expressed grave concerns about this pattern being repeated and escalating, as it almost always does in relationships. In the wake of the drama, the subdued couple agreed this was the best course of action. We decided that counseling would continue and that the wedding would be postponed so they could do further work *before* things were made final.

Two days later I heard (indirectly) that they were not, in fact, postponing the wedding but had decided to go forward no matter what. They felt God had spoken to them to proceed with their wedding plans, and they were determined to do so. Observing their slide into denial wasn't a new experience for me; however, it did raise the same questions raised in the first example. "Why don't people listen? Why don't they pay attention to the red flags that seem so obvious?"

There are two root causes for our stubborn pursuit of what we want despite obvious red flags.

1. The first is simple. We don't do what we know will be best for us because we *don't want to*. We prefer to serve our own comfort. Self-gratification is a constant temptation in human nature, and we're willing to deny obvious problems to get what we want.

2. We have blind spots regarding our motivations and rationalizations. We're capable of convincing ourselves of our noble and morally upstanding intentions while blindly overlooking truth and reality.

We can see these tendencies in both of the above

examples. At one point, in a rare flash of introspection, Candice told me she knew clearly what she was doing was wrong and destructive. In the moment of acting out, however, she didn't care.

The premarital couple spiritualized their reasons for proceeding with the wedding (saying that God wanted them to get married). On one level they really believed this was true. On another, when I asked them hard questions, they squirmed, didn't have answers, and cut the conversation short. They chose to bypass conventional wisdom and did what they wanted.

Everyone has blind spots. What is abundantly clear to many others can be obscured from oneself. Let's say a man named Jason gets angry and lashes out at his friend. In his moment of rage, he justifies his anger, therefore making his strong response seem appropriate in his own mind. The expression and impact of his anger, however, is much more obvious to those who are observing than to Jason. How Jason comes across isn't as obvious to him as it is to his friend. When the consequences follow (his friend avoids him or lashes back), Jason might be puzzled or righteously indignant. Sadly he doesn't see his own contribution because he has a blind spot.

Jesus warns against the blind spot in the following famous passage from the Bible. Matthew 7:3-4 (NLT) states, "And why worry about a speck in your friend's eye when you have a log in your own? How can you think of saying to your friend, 'Let me help you get rid of that speck in your eye,' when you can't see past the log in your own eye?"

Here Jesus warns the people about judging others and then refers to the tendency to focus on our neighbor's shortcomings while ignoring our own. Removing the log out of my own eye leads to greater clarity in my helping others.

There is no question that self-blindness leads to negative consequences. Unfortunately, when the consequences come, they are often chalked up to Satan's influence, and we sincerely pray for God's deliverance. What we fail to see is our own contribution, therefore making it more difficult to overcome the same type of problem in the future.

How then do we gain increased clarity and self-awareness? The first answer is to acknowledge the tendency to remain unaware. Simply admitting the human predisposition to gloss over uncomfortable self-truths leads to greater vigilance to detect subtle clues. Consider the following options.

- Paying better attention by listening more carefully to input that others offer.
- Catching subtle clues and inner contradictions and asking what they might mean.
- Humbly asking God for the light of his wisdom.

Numerous times the Scriptures promise us that God will give us his light in which to walk. Several Biblical references clearly state that God longs to provide his light and show us the way we should be, walk, and go. We are admonished not to walk in our own light but in his light.

The beauty of it all is that we can seek the light of God's truth at any point in the process, even after we have started down the road of self-blindness. It is a choice we make. The premarital couple will, no doubt, get married and also will, no doubt, encounter difficulties. Because they are people of faith, I expect they will petition God for help. This is where they'll encounter the fork in the road. If they're willing to learn, they'll walk through the circumstances and the pain, seeking the light of truth and learning about themselves as they go. If they simply want deliverance, they eventually will reach the conclusion that they or God made a mistake, and they will extract themselves from the unfortunate relationship, having learned very little about themselves.

Awareness comes to us as we walk in the light. In fact Proverbs 4:18 suggests that walking in the light invites the light to shine more brightly. "The ways of right-living people glow with light; the longer they live, the brighter they shine." In other words searching for the truth within brings greater awareness to see more clearly what is true.

Once you have established a willingness to search within, other practical considerations come into play. Let's explore some of them.

Listening

A big part of honest self-examination is listening well. When it comes to this, I have a pet peeve about current culture. By and large, people have become lousy listeners. Instead of exploring the intent of a message carefully and objectively, many people are receiving communication in one of two extreme ways. They either outshout one another in a competitive battle of superiority (attempting to prove who is right and who is wrong), or they carefully avert their eyes and respond insincerely in the guise of remaining "nonjudgmental."

In the end we're in danger of becoming deaf to one another. Maybe we have good intentions behind our chosen response, but the net result is that we're doing a rather poor job of truly paying attention. In the end we sacrifice the ability to gain new insights about ourselves.

I'm reminded of a moment when this became achingly clear to me. My husband was out of town on a three-week humanitarian/missions trip. While not common, this isn't a completely unfamiliar occurrence in our lives.

Generally the first week isn't much of a problem for me. I'm able to enjoy the time alone with a flexible schedule, meet friends for coffee, and maintain unchallenged possession of the TV remote control.

The second week is more difficult as I become increasingly lonely for conversation and interaction at home.

Since by nature I'm a people person, by the third week I'm counting the days until his return, feeling isolated, lonely, and somewhat depressed.

During this particular trip, I woke up during the third week feeling quite low. I made myself get ready for the day and set out to go about my business. It wasn't long before I encountered someone I considered to be a longtime friend. Knowing my husband was out of town, she kindly asked, "How are you doing?" I was relieved to hear the concern, and tears welled up in my eyes. Although I was a little embarrassed over being a baby about it all, I blurted out, "I'm not doing so well today." She looked down at the floor and quietly said, "Hmm. I'm sorry." After a short awkward pause, she went back to her task at hand. I walked away feeling completely unheard and therefore lonelier and sadder than before.

Honestly I don't really blame her. Maybe she really didn't know what to say, or perhaps she thought further questions would be intrusive, or maybe she honestly didn't have time to get into it. However, I felt lonelier than ever because my confession appeared to have gone unheard.

In general I wonder whether we are losing the ability to listen well to one another. Are we neglecting to search what is under the surface in favor of safer, more comfortable, less complicated relationships?

If we choose to go counter-culture and develop our

listening skills, we will hear more and therefore learn more. We will learn more about others and ultimately about ourselves. Others will give us feedback about ourselves verbally and nonverbally. Listening well means we pay attention to verbal and nonverbal cues and seek to learn about ourselves because we want to.

Listening well means we sit with a new thought about ourselves instead of quickly rejecting it. It means we entertain it and look at it from various sides and access what is accurate and what is not. It means we give permission to allow challenging truths about ourselves to arise no matter how uncomfortable it makes us feel.

Sometimes we are deafest to the people who are closest to us. Because we have erected walls and barriers, their input and observations become impotent and ineffective. Familiarity makes it more difficult to hear the truth because defensiveness and resistance stand in the way.

This robs us of a valuable resource in our journey toward self-awareness.

My husband used to say to me when we were arguing, "You think you're always right." I would protest, "That's not true." Granted, I am direct, and I speak my mind, but I also like to believe that I'm teachable and flexible. I flatly rejected his observation. In fact I'd quickly and dismissively shut him down with defensiveness and self-righteous protests.

Then one day it occurred to me that I occasionally felt like

I had hit a brick wall when it came to discussions with certain people in my life. Sometimes I experienced frustration with them because they seemed to be so confident in their point of view. I felt they were confident to the point of arrogance. One day I heard myself telling my husband, "They're just right all the time—at least they think they are."

Suddenly somewhere in the recesses of my mind a thought began to take shape. At the same time, I noticed the hint of humor in my husband's eyes. A little nugget of truth began to work its way into my consciousness. For once I resisted the urge to push it away and entertained the thought. Could this be the same kind of demeanor my husband was referring to? Could there be an air of confidence in the face of debate that is so much a part of my psyche that I don't even recognize it? I felt uncomfortable enough with that line of thinking to know that I was somewhere near a revelation about myself.

This process of allowing awareness to come is somewhat like unlocking a door, or taking a lid off something. It's as if our default mode is to compress and cover those uncomfortable revelations until we intentionally allow them room to wiggle their way into our consciousness.

Triggers

One of the best ways to discover new truths about ourselves is through our emotional responses. I recently heard a friend say, "Emotions are the lie detectors in life." In other words our emotions reveal what we unconsciously cover up.

I believe this is absolutely true. I find in my own life certain circumstances get to me, and I don't react well. From time to time things happen that trigger reactions that are, well, childish and embarrassing.

A while back I was saving toilet paper cylinders for a craft project. It was a suggestion from Martha Stewart. You cut them into 1-inch slices and wrap gross-grain ribbon around them and—poof—they're gorgeous napkin rings! I was collecting my rolls on the kitchen counter. After I came home from running errands one afternoon, I discovered my husband had crushed my precious cylinders to smithereens and discarded them in the recycling bin. I went from a sweet, loving wife to, um, let's just say, an "unhappy camper" in about five seconds. My husband was defensive but not terribly surprised by my reaction. Unfortunately he's been there before.

Afterward, when I calmed down, I reviewed the situation (with remorse and shame). My emotions had overtaken my rational thoughts. (Rational thought: *It's an empty toilet paper roll. There will be more where that came from…*) I quickly had surrendered to the emotional surge of resentment and frustration. You could say I was "triggered."

Everyone has emotional trigger points. They're different for everyone, but certain things get under the skin, and emotions respond quickly and intensely. Most of the time, it's an unconscious process. A certain look, a gesture, a negative remark, or an inconsequential event can bring a sudden surge of emotion that is strong and reactive.

Without getting too technical, the minor event unconsciously ties into something that's very painful, and a sudden strong response is evoked. When this happens, thinking becomes irrational, and outward reactions can be quite baffling to the observer.

I've reached the conclusion that this is a universal problem; everyone has trigger points. (Observe world history and the reality of war.) No one is immune to wounded places of the soul. As with any wound, there is a heightened sensitivity to stimulus as it heals. When the wound is touched or handled, it is as if we hit the roof, so to speak.

Among a mother's most dreaded words is the phrase "Mom, I'm calling from the emergency room." When our son Arden was away (far away) at college, he called me one day and uttered those words. Before my heart had completely plummeted to my toes, he rushed to assure me that he was fine, having *simply* sliced the tip of his pinky finger with a broken drinking glass mishap. Four stitches later he called to report that he was on his way home. The next morning I called to ask how he was feeling. He admitted that his hand was throbbing. He then casually shared that his Band-Aid somehow had slipped off during the night while he was sleeping. As he inadvertently touched the wall with his swollen and sore finger, he jumped off his bed with a scream as several volts of pain shot through his body. When the raw, wounded spot was touched, he hit the roof.

Raw, sore, and in need of healing, we're all in various stages of recovery. It's not that everyone responds in the same way. Some of us are screamers, loudly protesting with anger and indignation at the injustice of it all. Others keep it inside, taking the brunt privately and internally.

My friend Hope was raised by a mother who was a true Southern lady. I always have admired Southern ladies because I am not one. As well as possessing other social graces, they are gracious under pressure. From an early age, Hope's mother taught her to always keep a calm outward demeanor. She clearly recalls as a young girl, somewhere in the jungles of South America, sitting in a church service where her father was preaching when suddenly bats appeared, flying low over the congregation. Blessed with long blonde hair, Hope was intimately acquainted with the urban legend about bats having a propensity to get entangled in long hair. Her mother's nails dug into the skin of her thigh to remind her to keep her reaction to herself. She learned the lesson well that day. Thereafter she processed most of her triggers inwardly.

Inward or outward, vulnerable areas are exposed under certain stressful circumstances. In regard to the toilet paper roll incident, my bewildered husband wondered what was so evil about discarding toilet paper rolls in the recycling bin. He had no way of knowing he had inadvertently touched a much deeper issue in me.

Feeling discounted or trivialized is a trigger point for me. It's complicated, and it has to do with past experiences. On that particular day, however, discarding my project signified that I was being discounted, and I didn't like it all. My reaction was swift and intense. How dare he trivialize my project? Irrationally I jumped to negative conclusions, followed by more intense thoughts, such as *He doesn't care*, or worse, *He only cares about himself.*

Awareness is the first line of intervention. When a trigger point is activated, self-awareness brings it to a conscious level where we can begin to make good choices.

It's as simple as saying to yourself, *Wow, I'm really upset right now. I wonder what's going on?* or *I can tell by my breathing that I'm about to explode. What's being triggered?* Sometimes it takes time to get to the root of the matter, but with determination and self-examination, you can get there.

There is no substitute for a good "time-out," a moment to reflect and explore. The Bible tells us that the person who is quick to speak is foolish (Proverbs 29:20). There's something to be said for the power of contemplation and prayerful introspection. The writer of the Psalms said, "Search me, O God. And know my thoughts" (Psalms 139:23). The invitation was for God to examine the writer's mind and heart.

Conscious awareness brings choice. Having admitted that I'm upset, I open the door for choice. Will I respond or will I let it go? If I choose to respond, how will I? Will I speak? Will I act? Will I express my emotion? If I choose to speak, with whom will I speak? Will I stop and pray? Will I wait or will I proceed?

This brings us to a side benefit of observing our reactions more closely. The Heisenberg principle is a law of physics that states, "That which you are observing changes due to the observation of the observer." For example when subjects in food studies write down everything they eat, they end up eating substantially less. Their eating habits change simply because they're observing them. (As a side note, that's also why reality TV isn't reality; the observation changes the interactions.) Therefore observing myself being triggered helps me change my response. So if I'm open I can have a two-fold benefit: 1) I'll learn something about myself; and 2) I'll be more likely to change my reaction.

So many choices, so much responsibility—and, yes, this is the key. Instead of blaming others, as we may be tempted to do, we are actually responsible for our choices and our actions despite any surge of emotion we may experience. The responsibility falls squarely on our own shoulders.

The original flood of emotion may come, and maybe it can't be helped. We can, however, control the intensity and duration. In other words how we choose to express our distress and how long we entertain it is in our power. It's our responsibility—no one else's.

Let's face it. We need God's help and intervention. If we ask, he will help us gain insight, build awareness, and assert self-control. He also will remind us to humbly repent and learn quickly when we blow it.

It's painful to reveal the truth about ourselves. I'm insecure in certain areas. Sometimes I feel rejected when people disagree with me. Sometimes I feel stupid when my suggestions aren't taken. I don't feel accepted in some groups.

It helps to articulate your self-discoveries, either out loud or in written form. Sometimes you'll be able to explain it to the people who observed your triggered reaction and bring a greater and closer insight into each other's souls, but sometimes it won't be safe to do so. Choose what is best for the situation and for the moment. Write it down in a journal, process it with someone, process it with a group, or write a letter; there are many options.

Failure

For the longest time, I felt like I was a total failure when my more vulnerable parts were exposed. It's embarrassing to reveal our inadequacies and weaknesses. At the same time, failure is a universal phenomenon and inherently connected to our humanness. Why then do we resist acknowledging it?

Remember the car wash story? You might say this is an account of failure in my life. It's perhaps amusing ten years later, but it's not the way I would like to be known. Obviously I was triggered that morning, but I also learned some valuable lessons from that experience regarding behaving less admirably than I would aspire to.

I learned to stay in my car, no matter how unintelligent the other driver is.

I learned that winning isn't always as rewarding as it seems. I never saw the Eldorado driver again. Maybe I showed him a thing or two about discounting me as a driver, but what impact did my behavior have on my sister's assessment of me as a driver?

My very young son was in the car, and he was watching. He still remembers the incident. Enough said.

Somehow we have to come to terms with failure in our lives. Well, I suppose we don't *have to*, but we *may* choose to. Because we are human, and not God, we all will face it. Whether or not we want to admit it, no matter how competent, intelligent, beautiful, or admirable we may be, we all will fail. There always will be someone smarter, more intelligent, more beautiful, richer, and more admirable. Wait a moment, and someone will surely come along.

Acknowledge and learn. Let the acknowledgement be matter-of-fact and non-hysterical. This is where things often go south. Rather than calmly acknowledging the obvious

(*Wow, I made a big mistake*), we flip-flop between stubborn, defensive rationalizations and hysterical self-flagellation.

Either we maintain a false sense of perfection and superiority by casting blame elsewhere, or we feel hopelessly damaged and hopelessly flawed to our very core. Living in either of these extremes isn't helpful at all. In fact it gets us nowhere.

Failure has many lessons to teach us about ourselves if we only pay attention and learn. To learn something of lasting value, we must dig deeper than the surface and take a hard look at our motivations and belief systems.

A young wife, Kathy, called me to set up an appointment for couples counseling. She recently had discovered that her perfect (her adamant belief) husband Ken had been exchanging inappropriate e-mail photographs and explicit texts with a number of women. He had been doing this on a regular basis since before their three-year marriage. While he declared willingness to pursue counseling, I found it significant that she was the one who had called to set up the appointment.

From the beginning it was important to both Kathy and Ken that I know how wonderful their marriage relationship really was. Together for about four years, they could think of no relationship challenges whatsoever (other than the "sexting" discovery), and they happily shared that conflict was nonexistent in their perfect (except for one small problem) relationship.

Turning my attention to what had brought them into counseling, I learned that Ken had been involved in this behavior with various female acquaintances even during his engagement to Kathy. It had continued throughout their married life until Kathy, in a moment of insecurity, spotted the evidence on his cell phone one day. Shortly thereafter they ended up in my office.

Acting out in this way in a marriage is akin to poking your spouse with a big stick while he or she is saying, "Ouch." You know you're hurting your spouse with your behavior, but you continue to do it. It begs the obvious question, "Why would you stick it to your spouse in that way?" Most people in this position don't want to entertain this line of thinking, even though facing it is necessary to moving toward healing and reconciliation.

Ken was no different than most people. He was obviously greatly embarrassed by the revelation of his behavior and apologized to his wife. He adamantly asserted that it never would happen again. When I expressed doubt concerning his ability to carry out his promise without some insights about himself, he bristled. He believed that abstaining was a simple act of his will, and he was indignant at my suggestion that he needed to explore deeper issues.

Some obvious questions, however, needed to be answered. What needs was he meeting with the electronic exchanges that weren't being met in his marriage? If needs are satiated, there is no reason to search for them elsewhere.

What did Ken believe about himself and his marriage to justify minimizing his wife's needs and stomping on them? If you clearly know your choice will be devastating to someone, you are essentially saying, "Screw you" when you engage in destructive behavior. (Crudity intended for emphasis.)

What beliefs needed to change in Ken's thinking in order for him to be able to carry out his passionate promises to abstain over the long term?

We never got to the root issues. The couple dug in their heels, insisting there was nothing wrong and that Ken's choices were simple slip-ups that now would be corrected because he "knew better" and had promised Kathy that he would. In the end we had very little to talk about, although I swear I saw doubt in Kathy's eyes.

The couple's reluctance to face some startling truths about their relationship was a self-protective response designed to protect from great pain. In various ways we all go there. It's an act of the will to resist this kind of denial and to search for deeper truths. Ultimately we find that while it is painful, it is incredibly freeing to do so. There is great freedom to be found in calmly and humbly acknowledging failure. When we do so, we move through feelings of pain and remorse, finally emerging stronger and wiser, having learned from the experience. Of course sometimes there are devastating consequences to our mistakes. We must face and overcome these as well.

As devastating as it is, failure can be a powerful tool in building self-awareness that leads to growth.

Significance

If we were to narrow down the list of needs essential to our humanness, one need would come out very close to the top. It is the need to know that one matters. Knowing that one's life makes a difference and serves a specific purpose seems to be a conviction people cannot live without.

I do at lot of writing at Starbucks. I've heard a variety of conversations around me as I wrestle with giving words to my thoughts while gazing at my laptop screen. Sometimes I'm amazed by the depth of conversation that takes place in a public setting such as a coffee shop. It's not that I'm eavesdropping; it's that they're speaking loudly. One day the conversation beside me was about someone's journey to emotional health. I heard words such as "trigger points," "my story," "memories," and "anxieties." The counselor in me felt quite at home.

Initially I was only vaguely aware of the conversation, but suddenly one phrase came across loud and clear because the speaker raised the volume and intensity of her voice as she said, "I realized I wanted to stand up and scream, 'Am I important?' "

It is the universal question. It is why little children act silly in the company of adults; it is why people name-drop or brag or act superior; it is why others shrink back and fade into the woodwork. We want to know just how important we really are.

I'm a middle child. Middle children are known to have particular difficulty with this question, and I'm no exception. It emerges in group social settings, in professional settings, in ministry, in close friendships, in the intimate relationship of marriage, and in the roller coaster ride of parenting. *How important am I anyway?*

This question is really about significance. Deep in our psyche, we ache to matter, to make a difference. This desire seems to be implanted at our very core; it's a human need we cannot escape. It strikes me that it's part and parcel of our God-likeness (the fact that we are made in the image of God). Take away significance from a person's life, and health declines while death rates increase. We all have heard about the studies that indicate that retirement has something to do with increased mortality. Of course there are many contributing factors, but it isn't surprising, given our desperate need to matter.

The good news is that we do in fact matter. Our lives matter a great deal. From the very core of who we are, we were divinely conceived and planned for a specific purpose. This is where faith in a God who creates and individually interacts with his creation brings one of its greatest contributions and blessings. To think that I was conceived in the mind of God for a specific purpose and then created for that specific outcome with perfectly corresponding gifts and experiences is both mind-boggling and inspiring.

The difficulty comes in believing this is actually true. Many people give lip service to the fact that they matter in the eyes of God but hold the secret belief that they themselves (for inexplicable reasons) are exempt from this significance. As a result they spend a great deal of time and effort incessantly proving that they matter.

Unfortunately culture quickly steps in to define what makes a person valuable, and if we buy into culture's definition, we are hooked into an impossible standard of striving and failure. Fame, wealth, looks, and status are dangled before us like proverbial carrots, all beckoning as means of proving ourselves. Hoping once and for all to settle the question, we desperately strive for these things.

In the end family, wealth, beauty, and status do not deliver what we so desperately seek, and we're back to square one. Observe the rich and famous of our day. In large proportions they reflect discontentment, an inability to sustain relationships, and a desperate search for meaning that seems to have ramped up rather than abated. Apparently achieving fame and status hasn't delivered purpose.

But there's good news. There's a God who's not only the

majestic creator of the universe and all mankind but who also loves his creation and passionately pursues a relationship with humanity.

By his very nature, God must be perfect, intentional, and wise. He cannot be arbitrary, scatterbrained, or impulsive. If he were, he would not be God. He does not throw things together like I might create a last-minute meal with random ingredients (much to the dismay of my family). If he is God, his plan is perfect, always taking into account every possible factor and interaction. Perhaps we have heard it so often that it has become a cliché, but it's still true—God does not make mistakes!

Author and preacher Max Lucado uses the suitcase analogy to illustrate the reality of our lives. It's the best analogy I've heard. God packs into our suitcase everything we need for our journey—including genetics, experiences, and personality. He gives us a perfect blend of what we need to make a difference in the world around us, if only we will unpack it.

Unfortunately there is a tendency to want to live out of another's suitcase. The "greener grass syndrome" tempts us to believe that the contents of another's suitcase are much more exciting or desirable than our own.

A couple of years ago, our family traveled to Bangkok, Thailand on vacation. My sister and her family had joined the expat community in Asia, and we were privileged to visit family while also vacationing in an exotic location. Before the trip our son got a new travel bag from Costco. After a long journey, we were happy to find that all our bags had arrived on the luggage carrousel in a timely fashion, and we were off to the suburbs of Bangkok.

All was well until Arden began to unpack his bag. Out came a man's shaving kit (our son was about ten years old), size-ten men's dress shoes, and miscellaneous suits and men's clothing. He had picked up the wrong suitcase! Fortunately the Bangkok airport was wonderfully cooperative, and the situation was remedied quickly. Arden soon was equipped for our family vacation in Thailand.

Imagine for a moment, however, what it would have been like if Arden had tried to live out of the gentleman's suitcase. Picture a ten-year-old clomping around in huge men's dress shoes and an ill-fitting suit.

Ridiculous? Exactly. Yet isn't this what we often do or desire to do? We eye someone else's life suitcase with longing, constantly tempted to confiscate their belongings and make them our own, no matter how ill fitting they are. The outcome is unfulfilling and unhelpful.

We can find so much freedom and well-being when we fully embrace our own suitcase and the wonderful things that have been packed inside it for our life's journey.

Max Lucado also has written a delightful story about a town of wooden people called the Wemmicks. I love to give the book *You Are Special* to high school graduates because of its compelling life lesson. The Wemmicks have a system for classifying their peers. They attach shiny stars to those who excel and slap gray dots on those who underperform. The main character, Punchinello, unfortunately is a dot magnet, despite his best efforts to excel like the star carriers. Inferiority begets inferiority, and his life enters a downward spiral common to that of "wannabes."

Much to his surprise, Punchinello meets a fellow citizen who carries neither dots nor stars. Upon further questioning and revelation, he finds himself in the presence of the wood carver (the creator of the Wemmicks), who gazes lovingly into his eyes and says, "I made you. I think you're special." After this moving encounter, Punchinello finds that neither dots nor stars will adhere to him. Now, visiting the woodcarver every day, he is free.

The woodcarver profoundly says, "The stickers only stick if they matter to you. The more you trust my love, the less you care about their stickers. The less you care about the stickers, the more they fall off."

Even though the story is clearly a fairytale, the message rings true. We live in a world of stars and dots. Even when we manage to get pretty good at collecting stars, we tend to focus on the few dots that adhere to us. We may focus on brushing them off, or we may strongly deny their existence, or we may give up trying entirely and resign ourselves to life lived in the company of other dot people. In any case the focus is on the dots—our failures and weaknesses.

The woodcarver reminds Punchinello to live his life with a focus on this basic positive foundation. "I made you," he says. "You are mine. Trust my love." God, the master designer, made you. Not only does he love his creation profoundly, but he also has an agenda for you that fits with his whole plan. If God's creation of the universe is like a jigsaw puzzle with people being the pieces, he tailored you exactly to fit into the puzzle.

The poetry of the Psalms eloquently depicts this joyful reality.

Oh, yes, you shaped me first inside, then out; you formed me in my mother's womb. I thank you, High God—you're breathtaking! Body and soul, I am marvelously made! I worship in adoration—what a creation! You know me inside and out, you know every bone in my body; you know exactly how I was made, bit by bit, how I was sculpted from nothing into something. Like an open book, you watched me grow from conception to birth; all the stages of my life were spread out before you, the days of my life all prepared before I'd even lived one day. (Psalms 139:13–16)

While this affirmation seems like exactly the kind of good news the deepest part of our soul wants to hear, we still struggle to really believe it for ourselves. There are a couple of reasons for this challenge.

In our core beliefs, almost all of us have some degree of wounding. We have believed distorted messages or come to wrong conclusions all on our own. Psychological studies show that a child has formed a fairly definite impression of self by age five. It turns out that self-esteem isn't related to social position, family work background, education, or any combination of these factors. Young children see themselves from the reflections of those close to them, mainly their parents. How parents react to their children largely determines the self-images that are built. Children then live out what they believe about themselves.

I've watched popular fashion makeover experts Stacy and Clinton on television's *What Not to Wear*. This cryptic and not-so-subtle couple ambushes an unsuspecting fashion underachiever and benevolently bribes the person into updating his or her fashions with $5,000 and a well-documented shopping spree in New York City.

As a student of human nature, I often observe the underlying angst of the "lucky" victim. In most cases the recipients respond to the criticism of their long-standing clothing choices by insisting that they simply do not care about being fashionable. In one way or another, they insist that fashion is not "their thing." When they are good-naturedly harassed by Stacy and Clinton, their level of discomfort rises fairly quickly. It doesn't take much to see that they truly believe they are not capable of making fashionable choices, and even the $5,000 isn't enough to cover their unease and insecurity about changing their approach.

Clinton and Stacy somehow manage to guide the subject through the process, showing up at the moment of greatest anxiety and walking them through their choices. In the end stunning results are achieved and modeled. Upon seeing themselves looking chic and well put together, they display a visible shift in their thinking. The viewer observes hope dawning in the fashion victims' thoughts—*Maybe I can do this, and maybe I could continue to do this.* At least for the observable moment, a shift has taken place in their core belief about themselves. The degree of that shift will determine their future fashion choices.

We, too, have come to believe things about ourselves, and we live out these things as if they are written in stone. In some cases negative assessments of our traits were unkindly and untruthfully imprinted on us in our childhood with dogmatic statements such as, "You're too loud," "You're too shy," or "You're messy." Not only do we ardently believe these messages, but we also live out the diagnosis. Lies such as this must be rooted out and brought into the light, and we must doggedly apply truth in place of the lies. The reality is that a loving God created us for a specific purpose. Every trait is a blessing from him.

Exploring or "unwrapping" what lies within us is

necessary for us to gain greater self-awareness, which in turn allows us to pursue greater maturity and effectiveness. However, introspection for the sake of introspection and self-gratification can become obsessive and crippling. (Yes, even counselors understand this!) We've all known people who turn every conversation back to themselves. I'm sure I've occasionally been guilty of selfishly high-jacking a conversation and turning it back to myself, but there are always those lovely people who persistently do this. Sometimes I'm amused by some of these interactions. As soon as you disclose any minimal bit of information, such as "I brushed my teeth and made my bed this morning," they're launching into a sales pitch about their own toothpaste preferences and bed-making techniques.

To avoid becoming overly introspective, be mindful of the reminder in Chapter Three of Ecclesiastes, which states that everything has a time or a season. This truth applies to the individual process of self-examination. To the profound Ecclesiastes passage, I would add the thought that there is a time for introspection and a time to get over it and focus on others. That might mean setting limits on the amount of time given to self-focus and being intentional about moving away from it in order to focus on the outward tasks set before us. In that pursuit a rhythm develops in which the introspective times contribute to our effectiveness in the serving times.

How that works out practically will vary from person to

person. Some people I know get away by themselves for a specific amount of time on a quarterly or yearly basis in order to spend uninterrupted time reassessing reviewing, examining, and readjusting. Others work some time into their daily or weekly routine, possibly as part of their devotional or meditative life. There are also those who seek the advice of a spiritual director, life coach, or counselor. The logistics are not nearly as important as actually doing it.

The greatest contribution we can make in this whole journey of self-examination is giving ourselves permission. It is the mental assent to the reality that there is more within than meets the eye and that we are quite capable of denying truth even to ourselves. Obviously I *cannot* know what I do not know, but I *can* use mental discipline to open my mind to the reality that there may be more to learn. In that environment truth can break through and will set us free.

3 DEFINE VALUES

Need More Self-Discipline?

In a recent small-group setting, Lily hesitantly admitted that she struggled with an inability to quit smoking. Gaining momentum as she judged the safety of the group, she admitted that for years she had tried to quit but just couldn't kick the habit. She had tried every stop-smoking remedy known to mankind to no avail. In the last few months, she had succeeded in cutting back a bit, but her eyes mirrored the self-inflicted shame of being unsuccessful at giving up smoking completely.

The group managed to remain nonjudgmental and caring, most likely because decent, honest human beings recognize the universal struggle to be self-disciplined. As I sat with the group, my mind went to Paul's words. "The trouble is with me, for I am all too human, a slave to sin. I don't really understand myself, for I want to do what is right, but I don't do it. Instead, I do what I hate (Romans 7:14–15 NLT). In verse 18, Paul goes on to proclaim, "I want to do what is right, but I can't. I want to do what is good, but I don't. I don't want to do what is wrong, but I do it anyway." Apparently the inner struggle to bypass urges to self-satisfy in favor of doing the right thing is common to all of mankind—even as early as the first century when Paul wrote these words.

Many people would admit they need more self-discipline in specific areas of their lives. They believe they need this trait to accomplish their goals or abstain from harmful behaviors. Numbers of people wish they could apply restraint to various parts of their lives, such as their eating habits, smoking habits, sexual appetites, or destructive relationship patterns. If self-discipline were a dial that could be turned up—like a thermostat—it would make things so much easier. People simply would need to determine how to turn up their own dials, and things quickly would begin to fall into place. Those stubborn five or ten pounds that have persisted for the past several years would melt off with the newfound resolution.

Unfortunately the common method of applying self-discipline is the white-knuckle way. A resolution is made to try really, really hard and to apply every ounce of restraint to a particular weakness. Accountability partners are enlisted, fervent prayers for strength are offered, and firm promises of resolve are made to oneself and others. Society affirms that hard work brings results, and for a period of time, a valiant effort is made. Ironically, all the marvelous determination does not translate into success over the long term.

I think most people know on some level that the "try harder" method doesn't work but are reluctant to admit it. Doing so feels a bit defeatist and discouraging. If trying harder isn't the answer, then what is?

I recently spoke with a woman, Tina, who had lost all of her family's savings to gambling. Her problem recently had come to her "unsuspecting" husband's attention, although his surprise was a bit baffling, given that this wasn't the first time Tina's gambling had caused severe financial problems for their family. At any rate, Josh was very angry—make that very, very, very angry. Tina loved Josh very much, and seeing the very real possibility of losing him, she quickly jumped to attention, launching into the familiar process of convincing him that she never would gamble again.

Although clearly distressed and penitent, she made vows and promises that I clearly knew she could not deliver upon for any length of time. Tina desperately wanted to believe (and to convince Josh and myself as their counselor) that she was so thoroughly disgusted with herself and the pain she had inflicted that she never would engage in such activities again. She shared that she was so jolted by the family crisis that she had lost all desire to gamble and was now convinced that her resolve would last for the rest of her life. Unfortunately, despite her sincerity, Tina was mistaken; she was lying to herself.

Without drastic intervention, the likelihood of Tina's eventually going back to her addiction was extremely high and almost certain. White knuckling is a very short-term self-disciplinary tool and doesn't stand the test of time. That is why statisticians tell us that 90 to 95 percent of people who lose weight are not able to keep it off over the long term.[1] Sheer determination doesn't actually change behavior consistently.

I reminded Tina that she certainly had known she was jeopardizing her marriage when she covertly visited casinos and lied to Josh about her activities—otherwise why had she lied about it? From the beginning Josh had been clear about his disapproval of gambling. His preferences, however, hadn't been enough to stop Tina previously; there was no reason to believe it would be enough to stop her in the future.

If you have lived any amount of time with your eyes open, you most likely have learned that good intentions aren't enough in the quest for right living. The epitaph on countless gravestones could read, HE MEANT WELL or SHE HAD THE BEST INTENTIONS. Unfortunately resolutions do not lead to correct behavior.

---

[1] Gorrell, Carin. "Fit for Life: Keeping the Weight Off." *Psychology Today*. http://www.psychologytoday.com/articles/200201/fit-life-keeping-the-weight (accessed March 6, 2013).

Values-Driven Choices

What then motivates choices? You might assume that circumstances lead to responses in the way that A leads to B.

A - Circumstance ➤ **B - Response/Choice**

Tina had a hard day and therefore turned to her anxiety-relieving mechanism—gambling—in order to cope. In other words A (the challenging day) led to B (a decision to visit the casino). If that were true, in the future Tina would have needed to resist B (the urge to gamble) when A happened (she had a hard day). The problem with this logic is that Tina already had done all sorts of resisting and white knuckling, with only sporadic success. She was well aware that her temptation level was especially high on stressful days, but this awareness did not lead to any consistent self-restraint. In this she wasn't alone. Experience and research confirms that "A leads to B" reasoning brings inadequate change.

We are, in fact, driven by an inner value or belief system. Instead of two steps in the process, there are three. An event is followed by an interpretation that is followed by a response. The response is based on the interpretation rather than the event itself. A (the event) leads to B (the interpretation of A), which leads to C (the response).

A - Circumstance ⟹ ***B - Interpretation*** ⟹ ***C - Response***

Tina had a hard day. She told herself that she deserved some relief and that a few quick games wouldn't hurt anything. (She was lying to herself, but in the moment this is what she believed.) Based on her justification, she stopped at the casino. Even though all sorts of warning bells went off inside her head, she gave herself permission to stop because she really believed that *she deserved the rush she felt when she was gambling after a hard day.* It is the interpretation that must be rooted out, challenged, and discarded.

This is where the difficulty arises. Most people are readily able to acknowledge that their response must change. However, they are more likely to resist challenging their underlying belief. Doing so hits closer to home and at a deeper level and is significantly more painful to admit.

I met with a young married man who secretly had made some self-serving financial decisions that his unsuspecting wife later discovered. Basically he spent a lot of money they didn't have on some "man toys" and unsuccessfully tried to hide it from her. As a result there was big trouble in the relationship.

He was ready to admit that his desire for these objects had led to his financial betrayal. In other words he wanted to believe that his desire (A) led to his impulsive purchases (B). I pointed out that admitting to this kind of reasoning raised even greater insecurities for his wife. She knew that he surely had a desire for a lot of things, so the likelihood of a repeat performance was obvious. How long would he be able to resist acting on his desires the next time around?

In reality he needed to explore the underlying belief that justified his choices. He was much more resistant to this, but gradually he reached a greater level of honesty. In the process he realized the following.

His wife was "just a tad" controlling, and in return he resisted the idea that he couldn't do what he wanted with his money

He was more than a little angry with her for her outspoken assertiveness in the relationship. His actions were one way of evening the score (secretly). In effect his behavior was his way of passively aggressively saying, "I refuse to let you control me."

He suspected deeply that a man wasn't a man if he had to ask his wife before making financial decisions.

As you can guess, these beliefs were much harder to admit, and as most people do, he protested pretty strongly as they sank in.

Values and beliefs determine behavior, and behavior is always the determining evidence, no matter how much we protest. No matter how loudly I proclaim that I believe in healthy living choices, if I eat poorly and neglect exercise, my behavior reflects that healthy living isn't a priority over self-comfort. It's that simple. Behavior reflects belief.

People invest in what they value. They will go to great lengths to work hard, set boundaries, and apply self-discipline to accomplish priorities. Much of what we do and the choices we make are based on a value system. It's quite simple; I do what I value. Sometimes we are conscious of the underlying investment, and sometimes we are not. Along with that, recognizing and admitting the driving value isn't always easy.

I once worked with a client, Charlene, who had a difficult time setting boundaries with certain family members, particularly her mother. Her mother's demands and expectations were constant and relentless. Even though Charlene had a home, a job, and a busy life, her mother fully expected her to be available 24/7 to help with any need that arose, such as picking up a gallon of milk or changing a light bulb. She expected Charlene to drop everything and run to her assistance. To top it all off, her mother was hateful and mean in her interactions with Charlene, frequently putting her down and calling her names even while Charlene was serving her.

Charlene worked hard to define her limits and to risk being firm with her mother when her expectations were unreasonable. She found it, however, to be extremely difficult, and progress was slow. I pointed out that her choice to accommodate her mother was purposeful, with an attached underlying value system.

It gradually became clear, however, that there was one area in which Charlene had no problem at all in regard to declining her mother's demands. It had to do with financial requests. It turned out that Charlene had a very systematic approach to her finances. Independent since age eighteen (out of sheer necessity), she had learned to budget, save, and invest over the years. Her frugal living had paid off, and Charlene had been able to purchase her own home, give to charity, and invest in a growing nest egg. She was rightfully proud of herself for managing this part of her life. Even though her mother made frequent pleas for financial help, using punitive methods to motivate, Charlene consistently and firmly declined her requests.

When we explored this discrepancy, it came down to Charlene's value system. Disciplined financial management was a personal strength Charlene felt proud of. Because her success was affirming, it remained a high priority for her—more important than appeasing her mother. On the other hand, Charlene's personal time-management choices were not as important in her own mind as keeping her mother happy. When it came to time management, her mother's demands trumped her own.

Once Charlene gained awareness of this discrepancy, she was able to challenge her assumption that her own time-management priorities were less important than her mother's needs. It was an incorrect assumption that she lived out every day of her life with her mother. She needed to be challenged and to correct this assumption in order to influence her behavioral choices.

Why do you brush your teeth every night, even when you are dead tired and would love to just fall into bed? Why do you get up thirty minutes early in order to make time to wash and blow-dry your hair, even though you would love to spend a few extra moments snuggled into your sheets? Why do you go to work on days when you are so sick of your job that you'd rather have a root canal than go to work?

Why do you subject yourself to that yearly mammogram, knowing you'll be mercilessly squashed, pressed, and humiliated? Because your values drive you.

- You value having your own teeth.
- You value looking nice.
- You value financial stability—or the means to eat.
- You value your health.

Behavior Reflects Values

Ironically true values are difficult to articulate outside of behavior. Ask a person, "What are your values?" and he or she will give you a standard list: health, faith, loyalty, family, etc. However, his or her behavior will reflect the truth of what he or she values. Stated values may be evident in a person's life to some degree, but that person's choices will reflect where each value falls on the list of what's really important.

If you say you value your spouse but have an affair, you are not being forthcoming about the whole story. You may somewhat value your spouse, but you value something else more (perhaps attention, perhaps teaching your spouse a lesson, perhaps something else). Behavior has a purpose, and something in your belief system explains your choice. If you say you value your health, but you work ninety hours a week and decline your day off, you indicate that you love something more than your health. Words are indeed cheap.

So what is to be done if stated values and behavior do not align? We've already agreed that the white-knuckle approach is ineffective.

Congruency

The first and most powerful remedy is honesty. Speak the truth! Speak what your behavior reflects. "I guess I love the comfort food brings more than I love a healthy body." "I guess I don't care about my family as much as I say I do. Right now I care more about the gratification I get from my job. "

Admitting this is like jumping off the deck of a safe watercraft into the cold, deep ocean. We gasp reflexively as we plunge into the coldness. It feels painful and ugly, and even as we utter the words to ourselves, every instinct within us rushes to soften the blow. But wait—sit with it for a moment. Breathe it in. Let the dissonance and discomfort challenge you.

Living in a way that is opposed to stated values is "incongruence." In other words incongruence happens when outward behavior does not align with what we claim to value.

We are incongruent when we:

- Want to lose weight yet overeat.
- Say we are committed to being good parents yet scream obscenities at our kids when provoked.
- Claim to honor our spouse yet manipulate and control their lives for our own benefit.

Incongruence is a sign that something is misaligned between our behavior and values. It causes internal stress because of the underlying conflict. When this happens, a person's psyche works hard to find a way to rationalize, and the net effect is internal pressure. It's a bit like the effort of keeping a beach ball submerged.

High cholesterol runs in my family. My father and three out of four siblings have significantly high levels and have been on cholesterol-lowering medication for years. When I was first tested, my exaggerated lipid numbers became good conversation fillers. The numbers were so obscenely high that when I shared them people gasped and asked how I was feeling and were ready to call 911. Of course the doctors prescribed medication—big pills that were difficult to swallow and made me gag. I kept "forgetting" to take the medication. I felt a bit irresponsible and guilty about it and vowed that I would step to the plate soon (rationalization).

This went on for several years. At checkups the doctor would gently reprimand me, and I'd mumble something about trying harder to remember, only to remain unchanged. I was mildly uncomfortable (incongruence), but I assuaged my concerns with some pretty compelling rationalizations. I told myself that the doctor himself seemed to be somewhat ambivalent about the issue. I comforted myself with the fact that high lipid levels ran in the family, and I wasn't aware of any serious heart health issues with any of my relatives. I also was drawn to information about cultures where high cholesterol levels seemed unrelated to heart health (yes, I did find them). Feeling somewhat appeased, I went on my merry way.

Thanks to PPO healthcare, I eventually found myself in the care of a new doctor. This doctor seemed much more concerned about my high cholesterol. At our initial visit, he explained what would happen within ten years if I didn't get my cholesterol levels under control. In fact he explained it in graphic detail. I'm surprised he didn't pull out one of those plastic heart models—complete with pumping valves, life-size veins, and blood flow—but he made his point loud and clear. Potential suffering was in my future if I didn't address the issue. That day it clicked with me, and I believed him. I quickly moved past my rationalizations and confronted my personal value to live a long and healthy life.

I went home and took my medication that night and have ever since. No longer forgetting, I made it a part of my life routine and continue to do so. Suddenly I had resolve and determination where previously I'd had none. The difference was that I attached the behavior to my values. I value life and health. I value aging gracefully and maintaining good health as long as possible.

If you're not ready to change, be honest about it. Incongruence is inherently uncomfortable. We go to great lengths to rationalize our behavior to avoid discomfort. Ironically it's the discomfort that's needed in order to bring change.

Once you've become honest about your incongruities, determine what you really want. What are you willing to pay the price for? What are you willing to fight for? This might mean coming back to the basics of what you really believe and truly value. It's the foundation upon which life is built.

Growing up Spiritually

A discussion of values wouldn't be complete without visiting the topic of spirituality and its influence on personal growth. It seems logical that spiritual growth should affect our underlying value system, but does it really? What does it mean to be spiritually mature? I've often wondered this. How would I recognize a spiritually mature person if I met him or her? Furthermore how would I know when I myself was approaching spiritual maturity?

The Bible is pretty clear on the topic. Ephesians 4:14-15 says, "No prolonged infancies among us, please. We'll not tolerate babes in the woods, small children who are an easy mark for imposters. God wants us to grow up, to know the whole truth and tell it in love—like Christ in everything."

So what does spiritual maturity look like?

- Does it mean you have a "Christianeze" answer to every question?

- Does it mean you always have a calm, loving demeanor toward everyone?

- Does it mean you can quote a Bible chapter and verse on any topic?

- Does it mean you no longer struggle with anything more heinous and sinful than an occasional twinge of frustration when someone cuts in line in front of you?

- Does it mean you no longer worry about anything or get angry?

Many Christians mistakenly believe that maturity has a lot to do with biblical knowledge and doctrinal insight, along with outward conformity to whatever the current Christian community dictates. None of these things are wrong, of course. Biblical finesse and conformity, however, are not good indicators of maturity. Take a closer look, and you'll find that some people who outwardly appear to conform actually hide great self-absorption, divisive attitudes, and chaos in their personal lives.

There are four growth areas that might be more revealing of a spiritual maturity level. These facets of our walk of faith are in constant process, or a lack thereof. We choose either to move forward or to stay stagnant in one place. They are:

- Trusting
- Following
- Loving
- Simplifying

Trusting

The walk of faith is a walk of submission to a loving God who has our best interest at heart. Our capacity to trust God grows over time as we journey through the ups and downs of life, learning to recognize God's presence and love in every situation, whether good or bad. Trust means submitting to the truth that, when all is said and done, he is God and we are not. We grow in our choice to depend on him for everything. The degree of dependence grows over time.

Trust is the most difficult when we are in pain and can see no evidence of God's presence in our circumstance. This is the time when our faith is most severely tested. The temptation at these times is to take things into our own hands and seek resolution through our own resourcefulness.

We talk about God being silent. I'm not sure he is ever truly silent—not in the way a friend or loved one might be silent when we reach out to them. Sometimes my kids are silent when I text them or leave a phone message; they do not respond as promptly as I would like them to. I am left to wonder, *Did they get my message? What would keep them from responding? Are they preoccupied with something else?* Sometimes I even wonder whether I am less important than whatever else has their attention.

So it would seem when God is silent, like perhaps he is ignoring us, or is too busy to respond, or is simply preoccupied at the moment. However, if God is wholly 100 percent engaged and aware of us, this cannot be the case. Could it be that God is not silent but that we are not always able to hear him because of our limitations?

I'm reminded of the story of an elderly woman who went to see her doctor with the complaint that her husband seemed to be losing his hearing. He was failing to respond to her when she addressed him. He refused to seek medical attention, and she wondered what she could do to help him accept his new limitation. Her doctor advised her to test his hearing by asking him what he wanted for dinner. She was to pose the question from across the room, and if her husband failed to respond, she should move two steps closer and ask again. The doctor told her to continue to move closer and closer until he responded. Anxious to confirm her diagnosis, she launched the experiment that night. From across the room, she asked her husband, "What would you like for dinner, honey?" No response. She moved closer and again asked the question with the same lack of response. After the fourth time and about eight feet of movement, her husband finally turned to her and with exasperation shouted, "For the fourth time, I *said*, 'Pizza.' "

She had misdiagnosed the problem—it was not with his hearing but with hers. In the same way, the problem is *not* with God's failure to respond but our inability to hear the response.

I cannot make myself hear what I cannot hear. However, I can be open to the possibility that the problem is with me and wait patiently for the answer while pursuing better hearing and understanding. This slowing down, this waiting on God, grows with practice. It is like a muscle that develops with exercise. I trust that God is there and that he continues to speak into my life and circumstances.

Following

A follower does not *only* follow. He or she desires to become more like the one followed. This has to be true in our spiritual walk if any kind of growth is to take place. Jesus said many things about life and living and love and giving. Followers do what the leader says they should do, or they are not followers. If they don't, they may be curious observers but not followers. Jesus said if we want to follow him, we must give over our lives, our will, and our future to his will. No one does this perfectly 100 percent of the time. However, the amount of conformity should increase over time. You should be following more closely now than you did a year ago or even three months ago. Your Christ following inevitably should affect your demeanor, the way you treat others, and the way you live your personal life. Granted it is a gradual process with stops and starts, ups and downs. However, the criterion for spiritual growth is progress over time.

"If you love me, you will obey me," Jesus said. That makes it a non-negotiable mandate. Obeying Jesus means doing what he said. There is no room for excuses or rationalizations. Whether it is easy or difficult, allegiance to Christ requires it. Spiritual maturity requires obedience.

Loving

In general I find that people (including myself) are generally messed up when it comes to understanding what real love is. I'm talking about a 1 Corinthians 13 kind of love—love for another human being that resembles something in the neighborhood of what God's love is like. In its truest form, this love cannot contain fear, selfishness, manipulation, or vindictiveness. Naturally no earthly person can maintain a pure expression of love, but shouldn't the goal be to grow in it? Most people would say they desire to achieve a higher, purer love—in theory. When it comes down to it, however, it's freakin' hard!

The biggest problem is our incessant compulsion to attend to our own needs. Like drowning people, we cling ferociously to our right to extract what we think we need from another person. In the process we manage to justify, rationalize, and excuse our own non-loving contributions.

While marriage is only one expression of loving another person, it tends to be the laboratory where true love is severely tested most frequently, so I'll use it as an example. The most difficult discovery in a marriage is that moment when it becomes clear that mutual needs can and do conflict with one another. By "need," I mean a way of functioning that is least stressful and most comfortable for one's existence.

In any relationship that moment will come when one person's need stands in direct conflict with the other's need. In that instant, whether or not it is acknowledged, tension will erupt. Here are some examples.

- My need to be recognized by my peers as the life of the party conflicts with my spouse's need to avoid being the focus of attention.

- My need for inward processing conflicts with my spouse's need for clarity and verbal expression.

- My need for grace and mercy regarding my struggle with my angry outbursts conflicts with my spouse's need for constant kindness and affirmation.

- My need to make decisions slowly with thorough research conflicts with my spouse's need to act quickly and swiftly.

This is where the struggle lies. It isn't that we don't recognize the differences. The problem is that we judge the other person as being faulty, sinful, wrong, or just plain crazy. Then, having made that judgment, we go to great lengths to get him or her to adopt our approach. In that instant we leave the platform of true love, as we move toward self-promotion and need fulfillment.

Consider a married couple, Elaine and Kevin. They are mutually frustrated. Elaine is a super achiever who runs the family like a tightly wound watch. She is an extremely hard worker who gains satisfaction from her ability to organize and accomplish goals. Her home is clean and beautiful; her young child is well cared for; and her career carries prestige and accomplishment. She feels good about these things—except in regard to Kevin. He's not cooperating with her agenda, and she's extremely unhappy with him.

Kevin, on the other hand, is your basic nice guy. He's peaceful and fun loving, and because of that he has a lot of friends and receives invitations to many social events. His job is tolerable only because it meets a financial need and gets him from one weekend to another—when he can have fun with his friends. He enjoys life as well as anything that promotes relaxation and allows him to spend time with other people. He doesn't have a lot of complaints about Elaine other than that she constantly disapproves of him. From his perspective, she acts like a drill sergeant, complaining about everything and constantly correcting his way of doing things. He wishes she would relax and enjoy life with him.

Recently a camping trip turned out to be a micro example of the patterns that were developing in their relationship. As usual, Elaine had planned, packed, and made arrangements for the food, electing to pack the car for maximum efficiency. Even as she quickly and efficiently executed her plan, she felt somewhat resentful that once again she had taken care of most of the details. Kevin was happy to drive and was greatly looking forward to getting together with their friends. Upon arrival at the campsite, Elaine jumped out of the car, hoping to set up the tent quickly. She wanted to get the work done and over with so they could sit back and relax. (This is the way she felt most comfortable). To her dismay Kevin yawned and stretched and announced that he needed a drink after the long drive. He pulled two lawn chairs and two drinks from the back of the van, set them up in front of the fire pit, and sat down, hoping Elaine would join him. (This was his preferred way of approaching life). As you can imagine, it was a recipe for mutual frustration, and in typical fashion, a fight erupted.

When I heard them relate the story, it was the clear that both Kevin and Elaine thought the other person was unreasonable and uncooperative. Character judgments such as "lazy," "uptight," "selfish," and "rigid" were both verbalized and implied. Elaine was very frustrated, and with a lot of eye rolling and sighing, she accused Kevin of being selfish and lazy. In return Kevin felt that Elaine was uptight and unrelenting in her disapproval, which thereby justified his passive-aggressive refusal to cooperate with her rigid agenda.

They were in a battle to extract what they needed from each other. Elaine needed structure and order, and Kevin needed freedom from pressure and expectations. Their needs were at odds with one another, and their best efforts were going into trumping each other to elevate themselves. Before we judge them too harshly, it's best to remember that serving the self is the default mode of every person on the planet. It's the place where we start from the youngest of ages, and if we are not aware, we'll spend a lifetime perfecting our ability to manipulate, coerce, and extract from others what we think we need.

Growing in love means countering this compulsion with a grace that is greater than we are. It requires a Godly kind of love that grows in us. It is also a love that must be pursued—wholeheartedly and with intention.

There's no way around it. Disciples of Christ are called to love (1 John 4:7). This is not a fake, gushy, "Christianeze" sort of warmth that has no action attached to it. This is a raw, "I will do what is best for the other person, whether or not I feel like it, whether or not they deserve it, or whether or not it serves me" kind of love. It's brutally hard sometimes. When you're misunderstood or rejected or incorrectly judged, to love anyway means responding in a way that honors the other person's needs above your own—even when your own needs remain unmet.

Try it sometime. It's incredibly difficult to maintain, but spiritual growth demands progress in our ability to love others well.

Simplifying

The older I get, the more I long for a simple faith. If we were to graph the levels of simplicity of faith in most people's lives, it might look like a bell curve—from simple to complex (human nature's tendency to compartmentalize and explain everything) and back to simple again. In the beginning we start off with a childlike perspective—a longing for something greater than ourselves to intervene in our lives and interact with us with love. Early on everything seemed so simple—*I am undone, and love found me.* Somehow and explicably, the simplicity gets lost over time, and our faith walk becomes more and more complex as we insert rules, guidelines, and structure. Suddenly we find ourselves weary and exhausted, frustrated with other believers, feeling guilty for our failures, and disillusioned with God, who seems distant or even absent in all of our striving.

I suspect there are plenty of people who, after a strong start, have given up on it all. I hear there is a large percentage of Christ believers who live in quiet, self-protective faith outside of the bonds of traditional church life, having left the community weary and disillusioned. It isn't that these non-churchgoing believers no longer believe in a loving God, but that they reject the complicated trappings that only can be mastered by a few overachievers.

It's human nature to take simple things and make them complicated. It's our futile attempt to make sense of things by putting them into neat categories that make sense to our way of thinking. Basically the self imposes itself on the divine and brings it down to human understanding in order to feel a semblance of control. The irony of the gospel is that it's all about giving up control and surrendering to something greater and unexplainable.

Sometimes I picture my faith walk like a long drive in a sports car, and I am the car. I started out in the junk heap, broken and un-drivable. Hope came in the form of the Great Mechanic, who found me and lovingly and tenderly restored me to my original beauty. He overhauled the engine, cleaned and shined the body, and added extra torque and power. I was eternally grateful. My soul responded with dreams of new roads to travel and new destinations to pursue until I was roaring down the highway of life—shiny, bright, and well oiled. True, there was an occasional knocking in the engine, and once or twice I ran out of gas. There was also the issue of the sluggish engine when I was climbing uphill, but in general my systems performed beautifully.

Remaining grateful to the mechanic, I began to explore and test the limits of my engine, driving faster and maneuvering around obstacles until I was roaring down the highway. My destination seemed to be just over the next horizon, but inexplicably it never seemed to get any closer. Every crest of the hill revealed another hill. At first I had plenty of hope and plenty of power, so I kept surging forward, straining toward the destination. I pressed forward for a long time—a very long time.

One day it began to dawn that the scenery flashing by seemed strangely familiar and that the road beneath my tires was exactly the same road as the day before. With a jolt I realized I wasn't actually on a highway but on some sort of a conveyor belt, driving forward with dizzying speed but not gaining ground. With an even bigger jolt of surprise, I realized that just in front of the conveyor belt was a fast-approaching brick wall—tall, unyielding, imposing. I was going nowhere. Because I had no other choice, I abruptly cut the engine and sat before the brick wall and contemplated. What in the world was the point of all the driving? What difference had it made? Had it all been in vain? What difference did all the time and effort make? And the biggest question of all was "Where in the world was the Mechanic?"

Having no other options, I sat in silence and waited and listened. No engine, no movement—just sitting. I watched and listened for the Mechanic. Was it all my imagination? Did I manufacture his unconditional love and unprecedented affirmation of my being? Did I invent the Mechanic? Did I manufacture his loving restoration and encouragement? I sat for a long time and waited. Waiting certainly wasn't my strong suit, but I had no other options at that moment.

After a long time—a very long time—I became aware of a gentle breathing just behind me, and it gradually dawned on me that someone was in the backseat. Simultaneously I began to realize whose breath I was feeling. A wisp of hope began to dawn—the Mechanic was there all along. I had relegated him to the backseat, and still he refused to leave me alone, patiently waiting for my invitation to let him lead. In that moment I begin to realize that I had to trade places with him. I had to let him take the wheel while I crawled into the backseat. When I'm at the wheel, I encounter brick walls. When he takes the lead, the destination is new and fresh every day. The surrender that was too long in coming was sweet.

There are some simple truths that bring us back to the basics. This is in no way an exhaustive list, but it's a start. I encourage you to add the truths that you have learned.

- I am messed up, but love found me.

- I do not have very many answers. Even when I think I do, I often don't. However, God knows, and he will have the last word.

- God has an agenda and a plan for my life; he is 100 percent engaged in seeing it fulfilled in my life (way more than I am).

- If I trust him and open my eyes, he will show me what I need to see.

- When others wound me, it is because they are wounded. We are all wounded. I need every bit as much grace in my life as those who wound me.

- I must practice forgiveness every day of my life.

- Gratefulness brings happiness. I am grateful for the simple things: a cup of coffee with a friend, a good night's sleep, an expression of affection from a loved one, an uneventful, normal day.

Foundations

Early in our marriage, we invited a bunch of people over for homemade pizza. I worked diligently to prepare for our impromptu party. Overcoming my hesitation about baking with yeast, I followed the instructions to the letter—kneading the dough, maintaining perfect temperatures, waiting while it rose. Triumphant when it did rise, I rolled out the dough, applied the toppings, and waited for my masterpiece to emerge from the oven. I had timed it perfectly, so the guests were ready, soft drinks in hand, when the pizza came out of the oven. More than eager to consume this aromatic, golden-brown, veggie-and-meat combo, the guests watched as I set out to transfer the pizza from the pan to my carefully chosen decorative serving platter.

That was when trouble hit. I had forgotten to grease the pan. It turns out that greasing is a very important step in the process. The crust refused to relinquish its hold on the pan no matter how hard I scraped, pushed, and tore at it. My guests stood loyally by, watching me wrestle with my masterpiece, grim determination eventually giving way to resignation. Apparently we were going to be consuming crust-less pizza. It was a memorable evening. We ate shredded pieces of baked cheese with veggies and meat on top.

Who would have thought that one small, virtually unseen step of preparation would be so important? It boils down to a simple reality. *The groundwork is critical to the outcome.* The public, outwardly visible part of self is a reflection of the foundational beliefs and values in our lives.

4 TAKE RESPONSIBILITY

Take Charge and Relinquish Control

I have control issues. Some things just need to be a certain way in order for me to be comfortable.

My need to control became glaringly apparent one day when my husband, Werner, brought the chair cushions from the patio set inside when it was raining. Unfortunately they were already saturated, and the soggy pillows dripped a line of rainwater onto our hardwood floor from the patio door straight through the house. Unbelievably he didn't clean up the drips. When I came home a few minutes later, I could see the exact path that he took (which wasn't too straight, by the way). What kind of a person leaves droplets of water all over the floor and then sits down to watch football without even thinking about it? I, certainly, wasn't going to sit down until the drips had been cleaned and a few choice comments had been made, which generally implied incompetence and slovenliness.

To be fair, Werner's intent was to help me out with the household and keep the cushions from rotting in the Oregon rain. In retrospect it's also clear that the drips would dry quickly and be forgotten, whether or not I mopped them up. In the intensity of the moment, however, such rational thoughts never crossed my mind. All I knew was that any reasonable person (meaning someone who thinks like I do) would know what needed to be done and would do it.

What is clear now is that I was attempting to control my environment in a way that brought me comfort at the expense of others.

This is a common affliction. We desperately want to control our world. We don't tolerate discomfort very well and are willing to expend a considerable amount of energy avoiding it. The default mode seems to be an attempt to control anything other than ourselves first. It just takes less energy and effort.

There's a problem, though! We don't actually have very much control over things outside of ourselves. People, nature, and circumstances cannot be manipulated easily. We have far more actual control over ourselves, our behavior, our reactions, and our attitude. It just requires more effort— which is why we so diligently avoid taking responsibility.

An acquaintance, Jane's husband Brad, suddenly decided

he no longer wanted to be married to her. After seventeen years of marriage and five children, his bombshell declaration of lost love came out of the blue as far as she was concerned, and of course it completely devastated her.

Apparently Brad was a nice guy (loosely speaking), because he tried to protect Jane by not being very clear about his intentions. He gradually moved out and spent less and less time with the family. He became increasingly vague about his "new friends" and activities. He hemmed and hawed and said stuff like, "It's not you. It's me," and then in the next breath proclaimed that he had been unhappy for years (not so subtly implying that it was Jane's fault). He had sworn that the kids were his first priority and then moved into an apartment that could not accommodate any of them.

Devastated, Jane jolted into "repair" mode. Everyone has seen it. In fact most people have been there. If it's broken, it must be fixed. She begged and pleaded; she talked until she was blue in the face; she cried and appealed to Brad's good sense and faith in God; she tattled on him to the pastor and to his parents and to his friends, and to God; she analyzed him and tried to understand him; she went to counseling to fix herself, so she could tell him she was fixing herself. Pulling out the big guns, Jane called Brad one morning in despair, implying that if he didn't come and speak with her about the relationship, she might hurt herself. He came, but she saw the revulsion in his eyes.

In the end Brad increased his emotional distance from Jane. Finally, in utter exhaustion, she gave up. That is to say, she *literally* gave up. Sliding into despair and depression, Jane took to her bed. She contemplated the hopelessness of her situation and became paralyzed by fear of the future. She could do nothing but lament the brokenness of her life. Extended family members had to move into the home to help her with basic household tasks and taking care of the children. It was a very dark time.

Then somehow Jane inexplicably took a hard look at her situation and decided that her surrender to the inevitable doom was unacceptable. It was a turning point in her journey.

Realizing she had no control over her husband's choices, she turned her energy and efforts toward examining her options and making some decisions. Mustering her courage, Jane called a family meeting and reorganized the family chores and responsibilities. She called her parents and had them come for a visit to provide temporary help with the household. She started to tackle projects around the house that had been left undone for years. Reaching out to her friends, she called them and asked them to join her for coffee and girl conversation. She let herself cry for appropriate periods of time. Crossing a major hurdle, she called a lawyer.

Putting her energy into what she actually could control, Jane finally got it. She grieved what she couldn't change and became proactive about what she could. She was one of the smart ones.

Stuff happens. I know it's a slightly lame-sounding bumper sticker, but it's still true. Sometimes we have control over things that happen, and sometimes we don't. Too often we get mixed up about which is which.

The concept is easier to illustrate with what I call the Control Grid.

CONTROL GRID

	CANNOT CONTROL[2]	CAN CONTROL[1]
TAKE ACTION[3]	**Ineffective Striving**[a]	**Empowered Action**[d]
NO ACTION[4]	**Letting Go**[c]	**Giving Up**[b]

Throughout life there are circumstance that arise, and then there is the response to the circumstances. With that in mind, there are things we can successfully exert control over (1), and there are things that are not controllable (2). At the same time, we have the choice to act (3) or not act (4). Are you with me so far?

Take, for instance, the things we can't control. Unfortunately that list includes very many things, more than we would like to admit. Basically we cannot control other people, and we cannot control most things outside of ourselves.

We would very much like to think that we do have the power to control others, and we all have certainly tried since our earliest days. A key word that red-flags our own misguided control attempts is the word "get." "If I could only get my husband to…" or "If I could get that person to stop…" Unfortunately you really can't *make* other people do very much at all. If you "get them" to acquiesce through some type of coercion, the results will be short-term and feeble. You can invite people to respond to a request, but if it is to be a sincere and dependable change, it must be a willing act on their part. Too often we expend needless energy trying to get someone else to act, behave, or respond.

Go ahead and try to make someone do something. There are all sorts of tactics you can use, such as talking, nagging, wheedling, begging, guilting, bargaining—just to name a few. You may endlessly state your case, wondering when you finally will be heard. Depending on your personality, you might hint, ask, command, force, guilt, and repeat. Over and over you make your best effort—incessantly. Or you may signal your displeasure in passive-aggressive ways, becoming distant and unavailable and uncooperative while smiling and acting like you're OK with everything.

Then again you could try to get angry and hope that the other person will see your anger and recognize your pain, thereby motivating the person to quickly adjust his or her behavior in your favor.

Let's refer to the above table. If you try to act (3) upon something over which you have no control (2), it leads to "ineffective striving" (A). You may exert a great deal of time and energy on your mission to spur change, but it will be wasted and cause frustration for everyone involved.

On the other side of the grid is the opposite temptation—failing to control the things we actually can. That would be "giving up" (B). In this approach we discredit the options we do have, making excuses for our lack of action and taking comfort in the belief that we have no power. Most of the time self-pity and victimization quickly become part of the equation. Our attitude, choice of words, moral choices, demeanor, presence, or absence are examples of the kinds of things over which we have personal control.

Let's use the example of Tiffany, who feels lonely and disconnected from her husband, Jeremy. Tiffany is very much aware that Jeremy's preoccupation with work is contributing to the distance between them and, therefore, her loneliness. Logically, if Jeremy worked less, maybe she wouldn't be as lonely. Tiffany could direct her attention and energy toward "getting" (there's that word) Jeremy to work less and come home earlier. However, the control over that option being carried out very much lies with Jeremy.

While it would be completely appropriate and even advisable for Tiffany to ask Jeremy to adjust his schedule, whether or not he carries it out isn't in Tiffany's control. Let's say for the sake of argument that, for whatever reason, Jeremy makes promises but doesn't actually adjust his schedule. This is the exact place where Tiffany encounters the "control grid."

She could launch into a crusade to extract compliance from Jeremy (A, ineffective striving), or she could withdraw with coldness and distance (B, giving up). As many people do, she could swing between the two approaches.

Tiffany in fact has two other options. This brings us to the rest of the grid. Relinquishing the uncontrollable and making peace with this reality is "letting go" (C). While it can be painful, letting go frees us from the compulsion to make something into what it is not. There certainly will be sadness in coming to terms with our loss, and forgiveness will need to be applied. However, it's a much more sensible way of approaching the world and ultimately frees up a lot of energy to exert over what can successfully be influenced.

At the same time, there are almost always things that are within our control that can be further influenced.[2] This is empowered action (D) on our part. The tendency is to overlook the possibilities within our grasp because most of the time this requires something from us—a different kind of energy that must be directed toward ourselves. (Honestly it would just be easier if the other person *would just* change.)

Tiffany has options. What if she chose to think about her contribution to the distance between herself and Jeremy and her reasons for isolating herself? As painful as the realization may be, if her husband is unavailable, she still remains responsible for her own social network and interaction. After all she is an adult. To address that need, there are numerous options. She could join some kind of a common-interest group or volunteer somewhere or reach out to those who are already within her circles. This would be the "empowered" (D) option. In this way she would respond to the circumstance by acting on what she has control over.

Certainly doing so would require risk, effort, and thought. It also would mean encountering her fear of rejection, social anxiety, and insecurities. Therein lies the challenge—having courage to pursue and conquer the hard, resistant places within. You see, exerting control over ourselves is messy, risky, and painful—and we run the risk of failing. Besides it's just easier if others would cooperate and help us out.

Much of our resistance to moving into the other side of

---

[2] There are rare circumstances of true victimization in which empowered action is impossible. This is a state of coercion in which choice of response is eliminated by a perpetrator. In a lifetime this will be a very rare occurrence. Even then our mental response, attitude, and choice to bounce back remain under our control.

the grid has to do with avoidance of pain. Both "letting go" and "taking action" require something of us that often is painful. As mentioned, becoming socially proactive requires me to confront my insecurities and worries about fitting in and building relationships.

Abby was in her thirties. She was in a good marriage and had a strong relationship with her children. Her problem was with her extended family. Her brother, Justin, was a longtime drug addict with all of the issues that come along with addiction—a chaotic lifestyle, relationship drama, legal and financial issues, and ongoing neediness. The parents of the two siblings had made it their life's mission to rescue the needier of the two. It was nothing for Mom and Dad to terminate a visit abruptly at Abby's house in order to intervene in some crisis that had come up with Justin. Uncannily it happened almost every time they visited with Abby. The parents fully financially supported their son and had bailed him out of numerous self-inflicted financial messes for years. Getting together as an extended family required great vigilance on Abby's part, since Justin's live-ins and associates (who were ever present) had questionable moral character.

Realizing she was becoming increasingly resentful, and desiring a clear, un-conflicted relationship with her parents, Abby decided to talk things out with them to let them know how she felt. After discussing her intentions with her husband and trusted mentors, she gathered her courage and met with her parents. She did her best to articulate how she felt about the ongoing family chaos that centered around Justin's life. She shared her distress over being relegated to second place in light of the ongoing drama. She asked for concrete behavioral changes, such as their turning off their cell phones when visiting, and respecting Abby's boundaries when the extended family got together.

The conversation didn't go as she had hoped. Her dad got quiet and didn't speak. Her mom became visibly upset and let Abby know in no uncertain terms that her attitude was "un-Christian and selfish." Both Mom and Dad adamantly insisted they were doing the right thing by helping Justin, who so obviously needed their assistance. They also believed that Abby should turn over a new leaf and help Justin as well. Abby's mother made it clear that she believed that a good portion of the problem was Abby and her unwillingness to have compassion toward her unfortunate brother.

Abby had bumped up against something she desperately longed for but could not control—her parents' validation of her equal status in the family as well as their willingness to cooperate with her needs.

Even though she felt pain, she resisted the temptation to revisit the issue again and again, trying by various methods and means to get her parents to see things from her perspective and change, (A, ineffective striving). She also resisted the opposing temptation to completely walk away from relationship and avoid the issue altogether (B, giving up).

Abby found it necessary to accept things as they were and make peace with the fact that the family dynamics likely would stay the same for an undefined period of time— possibly forever. Since this was a painful thought, she concentrated on working through her grief (C, letting go) and finding a place of connection with her parents that accounted for Justin's antics (D, empowered action). It was less than ideal, by far, but she chose to focus on the things she could control and grieve the loss of those she could not.

When we approach life this way, we certainly will face pain. This is why we often resist doing so. Abby was left with the raw pain of realizing that she could not get her parents to respond to her needs in the way she longed for and needed. It hurt deeply. It was like being left with the hot potato at the end of the game. What do you do with it? It just sits in your hands, announcing that you have lost the game, while it burns your hands. Empowerment means dealing with the reality that the potato is yours, deciding what to do with it (quickly), and turning your attention to your hands as you consider what you must do to protect them.

This is one of our greatest challenges. It is natural and reflexive to avoid pain. If you move toward me suddenly and with intensity, my body involuntarily will flinch in an attempt to avoid possible approaching distress. It is a God-given reflex.

When we attempt to avoid pain, the temptation is to refocus on something outside ourselves. It is a way of diverting personal pain into something more like frustration and anger, both of which are much more palatable and empowering emotions. On top of this, we can almost always convince ourselves that our attempts to control others are productive and helpful, which makes us feel better about ourselves. Again this is a diversion from pain.

Why couldn't Abby just expect that her mother would try to understand and see things from her perspective? After all it seemed reasonable that a mom should do that. This kind of logic is the very reason why we keep trying so hard to *get* others to see things from our perspective. It seems reasonable to us. Assuming Abby's mom loves her very much, why couldn't she just put herself in her daughter's shoes for a moment and try to understand the longings of her heart? Surely if Abby communicated this clearly and eloquently, her mother would hear her.

Part of the problem is finiteness. We are trapped within our own bodies and minds. They're our only true frame of reference. What we experience and think is familiar and also makes sense to us. We assume this is empirical, meaning everyone else experiences it in the same way. If something makes sense to me, I assume it would make sense to you, if I could only communicate it adequately. What Abby wanted to express was, "It hurts me when you pay significantly more attention to Justin's well-being than you do mine."

The statement itself makes perfect sense, and the vast majority of people would be able to acknowledge and validate this thought, if they had objectivity. The problem is that Abby's mother does not have objectivity regarding the situation. She firmly believes that her suffering son needs more help than her daughter does and that Abby should see that as clearly as a mother does.

In the context of relationships, objectivity becomes greatly compromised because of finiteness. Abby's parents can't really hear her. They see the world differently and respond from their frames of reference. The minute she mentions her brother, all sorts of feelings and emotions are triggered, effectively shutting down their objectivity.

We are not only finite, but we also are emotional beings. Emotions play a large part in filtering what is heard and understood in communication. A successful resolution of conflict requires the following from both parties: hearing the other person, putting oneself in his or her shoes, and letting go of preconceived ideas. In other words a great deal of objectivity and freedom from emotional entanglement are required.

We've learned that we must be willing to tolerate a certain level of discomfort and anxiety in order to relinquish control.

We've also learned that we control because we feel anxiety or pain when we perceive lack of control. This is where faith comes in. Facing the fact that I ultimately cannot control many things leaves me restless and anxious. However, faith in a loving, caring God brings rest in the knowledge that things are in God's control. If God is God, he must by definition be capable and in control of my circumstances. There is a daily discipline of remembering that there is freedom to let go of certain things while at the same time taking hold of others.

Abby felt empowered once she began to act on her plan. She had moments of sadness when she was reminded of the unhealthy family dynamics, but she also was able to find freedom from the constant obsession and preoccupation with the things that were amiss with her parents. Finally able to turn her attention to her wonderful immediate family and supportive friends, she began to invest heavily in relationships that affirmed and validated her. Resourcing her faith, she found great comfort in the knowledge that God unconditionally loves her.

Living an empowered life requires something from us. It requires effort and a willingness to confront our own resistance when we feel ourselves slipping into blame and rationalization.

The greatest challenge of owning responsibility is acknowledging and attending to the attitudes and responses that we have the power to control instead of putting all of our efforts into what is futile (ineffective striving). For some reason the power we actually have seems obscured, while what others should or could do seems much more obvious.

While many people readily would acknowledge that they are contributing to a problem (it would be naïve to deny this), they often get stuck when it comes to identifying what that contribution actually is.

It might help to name some of the factors that we have the choice to successfully readjust. This is because they are internal mechanisms unique to ourselves over which we have control. Here are some examples.

- Our words, tone, demeanor, and actions
- Our expectations
- Perfectionism and our demand for it from others
- The need to be right, good, and loved at all times
- Forgiveness and grace that we extend to others
- Giving the benefit of the doubt instead of jumping to negative conclusions
- Compassion for another person's vulnerabilities, flaws, and triggers
- Learning from failure
- Pursuit of wisdom and education about what we do not know
- Trust in God for any outcome
- How much we expose ourselves to the hurtful words

and actions of others

This is by no means an exhaustive list, but it speaks to the fact that there are always greater adjustments we can make in nearly every situation. Therefore beware the temptation to proclaim, "I've tried everything!"

The most difficult part of being in a helping profession is wisely encouraging people toward a proactive stance in approaching their problem, instead of their resorting to the role of a stuck victim who can do nothing but stand paralyzed and miserable as they look for a rescue.

Sowing and Reaping

If we're going to talk about taking responsibility, we must discuss the Law of Sowing and Reaping. That's because taking responsibility means attaching what we currently are experiencing to our contribution. Once again human nature has a tendency to avoid applying this law to our own circumstances vehemently. Once again we are prone to self-blindness, forgetfulness, and rationalization.

If you've encountered God's grace in your life, you know that when it comes to your soul, you have not received *all* that you deserve. God provided a means for intervention, and you are released from the automatic and dire consequences of your sin. Be eternally grateful for that great and mysterious gift. Thankfully God does impart grace and bring more miraculous intervention and relief than we deserve. We are blessed to walk in this kind of grace every day of our lives. At the same time, he is a wise parent who allows us to experience the consequences of our choices so that we can learn.

What you plant you will harvest. In the Bible, Paul refers to this concept using strong imperative language. "Don't be misled. No one makes a fool of God. What a person plants, he will harvest" (Galatians 6:7–8). His words are adamant, with no wiggle room. It's almost as if he's saying, "Don't be naïve about this." Apparently Paul was aware of the human tendency to be just that naïve—naïve enough to deny that our current circumstances have anything to do with our past choices.

One of the clearest examples of this kind of sowing blindness that I encounter is in blended families. I'm certainly going to step on some toes here, but I'm willing to risk it. I'll use a fictitious example. Alex and Aubrey are in danger of splitting up—or staying together in misery. In a second marriage for three years, they have four children; two are Aubrey's, one is Alex's, and the two year-old is from this relationship. Aubrey's oldest daughter, Brea (age seventeen), is wreaking havoc for everyone with encouragement from her dad (Aubrey's ex-husband). For some "unknown" reason Brea vehemently hates Alex, frequently saying so and doing everything she can to oppose and undermine him. Blatantly disrespectful and manipulative, she successfully inserts herself between Aubrey and Alex time and time again. Add to this the ex-husband's encouragement of Brea's "expression of self" and his utter disrespect for Aubrey and Alex's values. This results in constant drama and chaos in the family.

Alex always has firmly believed that the man should be the head of the household and that he should lead his family with loving strength and wisdom. However, the family atmosphere is anything but calm and loving, and he takes this personally. He is beginning to believe that Aubrey carries a large part of the responsibility because she refuses to back him up by making Brea treat him with respect. Aubrey tries but feels completely caught in the middle of her obviously needy child and her frustrated husband. She is beginning to resent Alex's constant pressure on her to address Brea's lack of respect.

Alex and Aubrey are quite frustrated with each other, and they're beginning to believe that the other is to blame for the current situation. Of course they also both wish Brea would smarten up and get her act together.

A reminder and a wake-up call are needed for both Alex and Aubrey. This difficult family situation and dynamic were set in motion by a series of choices that began years ago, some of which predate Brea's existence.

- Each had chosen and married his or her first spouse.
- Each had a different parental approach to raising his or her children.

- All parties contributed to the problems in the first marriages.
- They both split up with their exes or responded to the ex's choice to split up.
- They failed to recognize the devastating effects of divorce on children.
- They both entered into a new relationship with someone who already had children.
- They both married again.
- They failed to recognize and acknowledge how difficult blended family situations can be for children (especially teenagers).
- They chose to have another child (which again affected the blended family dynamic).

This is not to second-guess their choices. Let's assume Alex and Aubrey have done the best they can, given their circumstances. Even so, choices bring consequences, and sometimes the negative is combined with the positive.

Planting and harvesting. Sowing and reaping.

That is not to say that we throw up our hands and hopelessly say, "We've messed up, and therefore we deserve this chaos." No. The acknowledgment of our own contribution is the first step in seeking solutions that take into account our own brokenness.

What if Aubrey humbly approached Brea and

acknowledged the impact of her own choices on her daughter?

What if Alex acknowledged that Brea in no way saw him as a father? What if he, despite his perfect family dream, let go of his need to be in charge, lowered his expectations, and dropped his insistence on Brea's unconditional love and allegiance?

What if Alex approached Brea as a non-demanding coach or friend, and let up on his absolute expectations of her? He could allow Aubrey, as her mother, to have more room to make decisions on Brea's behalf.

What if Aubrey and Alex readjusted their expectations of what a perfect, happy family should look like and settled for mutual respect and relative peace?

Taking these actions would be humbling and would require patient effort. This is how it is with taking responsibility for the things we have sown. Humility is an absolute requirement—humility and openness. In some cases, when gently reminded, people are willing to take responsibility for what they have planted. In other cases they are not. I haven't been able to figure out what makes the difference.

I have control issues, which is a common affliction. The fact that I am not alone in my struggle no way minimizes the responsibility I have to manage my issue. Every day we all choose whether we will take responsibility for our own lives in a way that leads to empowered living. Thank God that he has not left us alone in our struggle but instead invites us to enlist his help in letting go of what we cannot control and receive supernatural strength to follow through with what we can.

5 CULTIVATE RESILIENCE

Hard Times

My friend Jeanette went to the doctor for a routine exam. After gently probing the area around her lymph nodes, the doctor unexpectedly blurted, "What the hell is that?" Jeanette was startled by the cryptic words that changed her life forever.

Medical wheels were rapidly set into motion, and after a hectic week of examinations, tests, endless poking, and probing, Jeanette received the dreaded diagnosis of cancer with a capital C. Thus followed eighteen months of hell, much like the doctor's eloquent prediction.

I walked with Jeanette through some of those moments and closely observed her journey. I felt great compassion for what she was going through, along with the helpless feeling of watching someone you love suffer. Her experience also provoked me to introspection about my own life. After all, when someone you love goes through something like this, it brings home your own mortality. It begs the questions "What if that were me? How would I respond?"

Jeanette responded with enviable grace and a resolute determination to survive even the most impossible situation. I watched her wrestle with conflicting emotions: fear versus hope, despondency versus confidence, weariness versus elation, and resignation versus determination. She focused on the goal—remission of the cancer and a normal life as a wife, mother, grandmother, and business owner. Walking through the ups and downs, she determined to make it through gracefully. I observed her with admiration.

Another acquaintance—let's call her Betty—experienced the ultimate marital betrayal many years ago. Her husband cheated on her with a close family friend. Forty years later she has not gotten over it. She has spent forty years in bitter, unyielding resentment. The story of her rejection becomes quickly apparent in every interaction she has, every choice she makes, and almost every conversation in which she engages. It is unpleasant to encounter and painful to observe.

A vast difference emerges between the two responses to devastating circumstances and monumental challenges. The responses are so different that they bring up a compelling question. What does it take to bounce back from traumatic life events intact and be ready to move on healthy and whole?

Along this same line of questioning, scientists have asked, "What contributes to resilience in humans?" Resilience by definition is "the capability of a strained body to recover its size and shape after deformation caused especially by compressive stress" (Merriam-Webster). In the context of these pages, it refers to after-stress recovery to reach a state that is close to the original state before the upheaval occurred.

Why do some children who are severely abused grow up to be productive, strong, centered people who pass on a completely different legacy to their own offspring, while others never overcome childhood trauma and engage in chronic, addictive, self-destructive behaviors that are resistant to intervention? When I was in labor with our son, I was joyfully visiting with a roomful of friends in the hospital until about five minutes before I gave birth. Watching the monitor out of the corner of my eye, I observed the contractions rising and falling as they increased in length and intensity—on paper. Physically I felt nothing except anticipation and expectation.

Even now I sigh with the beauty and marvel of it all—I'm referring to the capabilities of medical science (even though the birth itself was, of course, beautiful too).

My utter gratefulness for the miracle of modern medicine speaks to this truth—pain seeks relief. God created us this way. At its most basic core, the body seeks to avoid pain. If a sharp object advances toward us rapidly, our recoil response is instinctive. God graciously has bestowed upon us basic protective measures to potential harm.

Only in extreme examples of emotional distress and pathology do people intentionally seek pain, but even in that case, it could be argued that this kind of twisted pursuit is a misguided attempt to soothe deeper, even more intense emotional pain and trauma.

Even so, the truth is that sometimes life is painful. At the risk of sounding overly simplistic, God seems to allow pain into our lives in relative frequency. Bad things happen to good people who have a good God, and when they happen, it hurts.

The list of events that can generate pain is long.

Broken relationships

Infidelity

Rebellious or troubled children

Betrayal by one who uses us in self-serving ways

Loss and death

Illness and physical difficulty

Anxiety and depression

Financial hardships

When we face the prospect of pain, it seems logical to find

ways to avoid it. If we are left to our first inclinations, escape becomes the first and foremost priority. Escape can take various forms, many of which lead us down false paths that do not solve the original problem.

- Engaging in substance abuse and other addictions
- Unnecessarily abandoning relationships
- Over-spiritualizing and failing to face reality
- Blaming and showing bitterness toward others
- Avoiding or running away—physically, emotionally, spiritually

Obviously these attempts at relief do not solve the problem and often lead to additional problems.

Ironically, even though we desperately try to avoid suffering, it is also one of the greatest catalysts to personal growth. For whatever reason, negotiating painful circumstances plays an essential role in strengthening character and developing wisdom. Caught between these forces, we are left to choose which path to embrace.

While hard times *can* lead to personal growth, it's not *always* the outcome. What I mean is that there's a relationship between pain and growth, but the one does not always lead to the other. As is the case with my friend Betty, it's possible to encounter painful experiences but never learn a thing from them.

This reality was recently brought home to me in a very

powerful way. My parents—especially my father—are a potent example of "overcomers" who became stronger and more effective because of the trauma they encountered in their lives. Both my father and my mother know the suffering of war and trauma in a very personal way. In the aftermath of World War II, my father, at age thirteen, was transported from Poland to Siberia (a thirty-day trip) in a boxcar that was filled to standing-room-only capacity with war refugees. Surviving the journey was a miracle in itself because food and water weren't provided during the excruciating trip. The occupants of the train had to fend for themselves in impossible circumstances.

Upon arrival in Siberia, my dad was put to work in a brick factory while suffering from malnutrition and enduring frigid temperatures in the harsh climate.

This became his life for three years. If being cold and hungry while making bricks during the nightshift in a prison camp wasn't traumatic enough, he also was assigned the task of transporting cartloads of dead bodies and burying them in mass graves. Most of us could not conceive of such hardship.

How did this affect him? Well, I remember he was always tender in his relationship with God. I remember his faith in God seemed to be the most important thing in his life. I remember that he prayed and believed in God in every circumstance. Many times he comforted my own ominous concerns with the words "You'll see. It'll be OK. God will help you." Although I didn't realize it at the time, he was absolutely right.

I never detected any bitterness toward those who had imposed these hardships on him. "It was wartime," he would say. "War is a terrible thing. I don't blame the people." If you could meet my dad, you would soon see that he is at peace with himself and with God.

A few months ago, I had the privilege of traveling to Tallinn, Estonia, where I met some remarkable women. One day over lunch, I bonded with Nadia, a young woman whose heritage sounded remarkably similar to mine, except for some major differences in the outcome.

Without going into a great deal of political and historical detail, it turns out that many people in that part of Europe know someone who was transported to Siberia at the same time that my father was. This young woman shared that her father also been taken there as a prisoner of war, at the age of seven. Nadia spoke of the great fear and trauma he had experienced at such a young age. She shared the compelling image of this bewildered frightened child disembarking from the train while politically brainwashed locals threw rocks at him. This seven-year-old spent his first night in Siberia trembling in fear for his life in the woods.

Nadia's dad hadn't overcome the trauma and to this day is greatly affected by it. She shared that her father is a raging alcoholic who has spent most of his life drinking away his memories while taking out his anger about past experiences on his family. She shared that her spiritual conversion to Christianity had so enraged him that he beat her severely. Social services had to intervene and rescue her from further harm.

It occurred to me that this poor man was still hiding and trembling in the woods, so to speak. Remarkably, Nadia shared how her faith had challenged her to reach out to him in his pain and establish a relatively stable relationship with him.

It wasn't until later that day that it occurred to me that while our fathers had experienced similar trauma, the outcome was vastly different. As I contemplated that, I realized that the difference was a choice each man made in his life. It was a choice about how to respond to the incomprehensible challenges that life brings.

One man (boy) tapped into a strong faith in a good God of redemption, while the other allowed fear and rage to take hold. One embraced forgiveness, the other bitterness. One passed on a legacy of tenderness in the midst of trial, while the other imposed fear and intimidation on those closest to him.

Somewhere along the way, a decision is made, either to face the trial intentionally and maximize its growth potential, or to avoid, suppress, and ultimately deteriorate. For us to allow trials to strengthen us, we must make a conscious decision to override our natural tendency to run and instead face the issue courageously. We definitely need God's help, but our hearts must give him permission to do that work, despite the pain.

Jesus referred to the phenomenon of growth under duress. Using fruit as an example, he highlighted the relationship between the health of the vine and the pruning process. "I am the Real Vine and my Father is the Farmer. He cuts off every branch of me that doesn't bear grapes. And every branch that is grape-bearing he prunes back so it will bear even more" (John 15:1–3).

The idea of being "pruned" is not a pleasant thought. I would rather God periodically employ some sort of cosmic anesthesia in order to do his work in us—adjusting, enlarging, removing what doesn't fit or repairing, what has been damaged. Then we could wake up and hit the ground running without memory of the procedure, while feeling better and functioning more effectively. Unfortunately it doesn't work this way. Perhaps it has something to do with the fact that without effort on our part, we would atrophy and become more and more dependent rather than partner with God in impacting the world.

How well we learn, or how much we grow from adversity, has very much to do with a choice we make in the wake of the obstacles that come our way.

If we choose the growth path, we will one day be

surprised to realize that somewhere, somehow, inexplicably, we have progressed, we have learned. We are forever changed. Upon the realization we are grateful. Although we never would choose to walk through the trial, we are eternally grateful for the outcome.

When difficult things come your way—no matter what happens—choose to live, choose to let go, choose to forgive, choose to move on, choose to learn, and you will certainly bear good fruit.

Take Back Control

When really bad things alter our lives, one of the most common challenges is the feeling of loss of control. Helplessness and utter devastation are likely to follow.

We might internally say something like, *Really bad things are happening. I didn't ask for this; I didn't choose this; I don't deserve this—and yet it's happening, and I can't do anything about it. This isn't what I wanted for my life.*

Consider the woman who becomes aware that her husband is involved with someone else, or the person who receives a dreaded diagnosis that requires treatment that would damage a healthy body in any other circumstance. Instantly life is changed, resulting in a series of very unpleasant events that must now be navigated and endured.

The temptation would be to resort to escape tactics, like those of a child. It might involve some sort of running and hiding, begging God and everyone for deliverance from the circumstance. In truth a response like this is fine in the initial trauma of devastation. However, if the response isn't held in check, it morphs into a victim mentality over time that quickly becomes anger and resentment. This is because we cannot make God or others do what we want them to do at any given moment.

Unfortunately (or maybe fortunately), we only have control over ourselves. We have control over *our own* behaviors, *our own* words, *our own* ability to ask for help, *our own* vulnerability with others. When we exert control over these things, we step out of the victim stance and into a proactive stance that, in the end, is vastly more empowering.

"That's not easy," you may protest. "You couldn't possibly know what it's like unless you've been through it." The ease of exerting control over ourselves cannot be a determining factor in the choice. Let's acknowledge that it is monumentally, enormously difficult to move from a victim stance to one of self-control. Even so the alternative (pain avoidance) is unacceptable and keeps you stuck in one place, which perpetuates your pain.

Remind yourself that in life, the times when we have absolutely no control are rare indeed. If you search diligently, you'll always find some area over which you can, in fact, exert some control.

I spoke with a woman, Stacy, who was slowly and

anxiously becoming aware that her husband was drawing away from her. His emotional disconnection and dismissal was becoming more and more obvious. Although he didn't openly disclose his state of mind and heart, it was becoming more and more apparent that if the choice were his, their relationship would be over.

As would be expected, this brought a great deal of fear and anxiety to Stacy, who desperately wanted to restore the relationship. Her default response was to try as much as possible to appease him and convince him that he was making a mistake. She tried to be on her best behavior, pleasing him as best she could without his open disclosure of what he actually wanted from her.

She entered into a certain amount denial of the situation by explaining his emotional distance as temporary confusion due to his struggle with depression, which (she told herself) eventually would pass.

The realities of the situation, however, became more and more apparent as he continued to withdraw from her. Eventually she chose to face the blatant truth and consider what she needed to do to take care of herself and survive. She learned to engage in self-comforting behaviors and increase her self-care. She reached out to friends and acquaintances. She also began to imagine what her life would be like without her husband. What would she do? Where would she go? Though the situation was painful, she was able to acknowledge that her life would continue with or without him and that she would thrive no matter the end result, even if it were a long, grief-filled journey.

Even though Stacy was still in a great deal of pain over the increasing emotional distance in her marriage, hope began to dawn when she realized she would survive. Hope is a powerful factor in bouncing back from trauma. When hope is lost, people give up, and when they give up, the prospects for recovery are dismal. However, with hope, people find the strength to keep moving forward and reaching for the goal of healing and recovery.

Forgive

As discussed in previous chapters, the other side of taking control is letting go of what we cannot control. In a resilient life, recovering from traumatic events requires one crucial piece. That piece is forgiving, and true freedom cannot be found without it. Forgiveness is the act of letting go of anger and releasing rights to retribution and revenge. It means letting go of a debt. It's complicated, confusing, and gut wrenching. Ultimately it requires supernatural intervention when it seems beyond possible.

C.S. Lewis put it well when he said, "Forgiveness is a wonderful thing unless you're asked to do it."

When it comes to our relationships with one another, things can go wrong. Sadly none of us is exempt from inevitable clashes at some point in our lives—that is, unless you live alone on a deserted island. Sometimes the deterioration in a relationship is gradual, one that dawns slowly and painfully. Other times it comes out of the blue and is shocking, abrupt, and devastating. Sometimes it's both—a gradual sense of unease and tension, followed by an abrupt explosion or termination of connection.

A friend recently shared her devastating journey with me. The details were unique but the story familiar. Beth spoke of a very difficult marriage with a long history of conflict, tension, rejection, and unspoken suspicions about her husband, Craig. Despite the pain, long ago she had made a firm resolution to move forward in the relationship for the sake of her faith and her children, and she tried to make the best of a difficult situation.

Out of the blue, Beth's suspicions were confirmed one day when Craig abruptly announced that he was leaving her for someone else. Along with this revelation, Craig came clean about his hidden sexual addiction and resulting choices, which clearly dishonored the relationship. The disclosures came wrapped in layers of abandonment and rejection, and Beth was left feeling devastated and numb. All she could think was, *I was putting up with Craig's junk because I thought it was the right thing to do, and now he has the nerve to abandon me after having deceived and dishonored me?*

As Beth shared her story, I felt her indignation to the

depths of my soul. What Craig had done to dishonor her was just wrong.

This is the deepest kind of wounding. It is a rejection and betrayal right down to the very roots of the soul. From Beth's perspective, she was now being kicked to the curb after what had seemed like a lifetime of giving above and beyond the norm. How in the world could Beth even begin to think of forgiving her narcissistic husband? Through his own selfishness, he set into motion a series of events that will result in ongoing pain and devastation not only for Beth but also their children and extended families. It seems almost inconceivable to let him off the hook.

I know approximately how she feels. My husband has been a pastor for thirty-two years, and we've had our share of church drama. As anyone in church leadership knows, when you deal with people, you deal with broken humanity. Add to that the fact that the leaders themselves wrestle with their human weakness every day. Then add relational awkwardness on everyone's part, and you have recipes for difficulty.

We recently encountered a situation in which a family, the Smiths, who had been a great blessing to our church, couldn't see eye to eye with the church leadership regarding some organizational issues. The Smiths are great people. We had socialized and worked side by side with them in peaceful harmony and mutual admiration for a long time. In hindsight it appears they must have gradually lost their confidence in the church leadership over a period of time, but at the time it seemed they abruptly had begun to disagree with every decision that was made. Out of the blue (apparently), they became critical and argumentative and chose to protest in a way that was designed to engage other members of the congregation in debate and further discussion of the issues.

I have no doubt the Smiths prayed diligently about their approach and felt justified in their stance. Further I neither wish to be the victim nor feel superior by making judgments about them. However, their choice to vocally discredit us with others hurt badly, and it felt largely like an attack. Disbelief, incredulity, and indignation vied for attention as the pieces emerged over several weeks. Since a commitment to forgiveness is a core value of my life, however, thoughts of it became prevalent from my first inkling of unease. In the beginning I wrestled with the conflict between my resentment and my value system, and there were moments when it seemed my emotions were winning.

On our best days, living as a forgiver will stretch us to our very core. The struggle will be greater, however, if we misunderstand the concept of forgiveness. Essentially forgiveness is simply releasing another from a debt. It means letting go of a desire for payment or payback for a wrong that was committed.

The problem lies at the very root of our being and nature. A desire for "fairness" seems to be built into our psyche, where we live in a currency-based default mode. In other words we believe somebody needs to pay. For that reason we continually revert back to retribution, blame, vengeance, and justice. *Whose fault is it anyway? Who is to blame? Who must pay?* Tempted to relentlessly pursue the answers to these questions, we seek to determine "who is right" and "who is wrong." Unfortunately this kind of debt-determination unwittingly sets us up in the judge's seat. In our own judgment, we are uncanny in our ability to come to the conclusion that we are right and others are wrong, which gives us permission to take pride in our "rightness."

We then take the next inevitable step—seeking to extract payment from the guilty one. This is exactly what un-forgiveness is about. Un-forgiveness holds the one who has wronged us close to our psyche, as we demand justification and retribution. This relentless pursuit of repayment is the core of un-forgiveness.

Believing we are owed, we wait in vain for payback. Unfortunately it rarely comes, at least not in a way that seems sufficient. Even when the other party makes attempts (by offering an apology or an acknowledgment, for example), it often seems inadequate in the face of our pain. Explanations, in the rare instances that they come, seem trite and frivolous. We are tempted to continue to replay the wrong over and over in our minds, believing the other is in danger of getting away with it if we do not vigilantly keep score. Left with the consequences of what was inflicted upon us, we feel it's wrong that the other person can continue on with life, unaffected and oblivious to our pain. It assaults our sense of justice.

Because the wounding counts as an unpaid debt, we feel it is necessary to hang on to the offense and replay it again and again. Like a careful accountant who painstakingly keeps record of receivables to avoid being swindled, we carefully tabulate the injustice and remind others and ourselves of the injustice again and again. Wrongly assuming that careful accounting will protect us from further vulnerability, we become hard and unyielding, eventually viewing the entire world as a place that will get the best of us if we let down our guard.

If you've lived long enough, you may know of such an individual, or you yourself may be one. In the latter case, you unfortunately know there's a catch to the meticulous recordkeeping. Hanging on to the offense does little to extract payment. The debt isn't satisfied that way. In fact it seems to grow larger over time. The world becomes more and more ominous and ultimately isolating. Energy is expended in replaying and reliving the past. Soon self-protectiveness and hardness set in.

Living eventually becomes a reflexive process, and it's necessary to protect yourself from further victimization. In the end the debt is never satisfied, and you come to believe that God is unfair and no longer on your side. In the end life stops and cannot move forward.

Forgiveness, however, takes a different path. It is a path that at first glance may seem unfair and contrary to your sense of justice. God, however, clearly mandated forgiveness because it ultimately frees a person to move forward in life, unhindered by preoccupation with things that are not in our control.

In its purest form forgiveness is relatively simple; it is a release from debt. No matter what hardship I believe you have imposed on me, you do not owe me anything. You are free. There are no ties between us, and you do not have to answer to me, pay me, or make things right. I release you from any debt.

This approach requires a lifestyle commitment to forgiveness and release from debt as a way of life—a new worldview. At its core it states, "God is the only judge, and I am certainly not God. My own perspective is skewed and tends to be largely self-serving. Therefore, when I am hurt, I will acknowledge the hurt and turn my attention toward whatever is needed for healing. I will release the object of my hurt into God's care. I will try to understand what I need to in order to move on. Some things, however, I never will understand because they're simply out of the realm of my comprehension." In the end there is great freedom in this approach.

Forgiveness now takes on a new spin. It takes us off the judge's bench and puts us squarely into the unknown. We cannot judge another; only God knows the heart.

Let there be no confusion. There are some things that forgiveness is not. Forgiveness does not mean excusing someone's behavior. It does not condone or minimize actions, insults, slights, or wrongs. It doesn't say, "It doesn't matter," "It's all OK," "It's not important," "I deserved it," or "It was no big deal." It also does not ignore bad behavior, which can propel the injured party from a place of vulnerability to one of victimization.

Forgiveness does not always mean that we release another from the consequences of his or her actions. Natural and logical consequences follow behavior. In most cases we are not obligated to stand in the way of such natural consequences. If I do something illegal, the legal system has consequences in place that will be set in motion after I make the choice to break the law. Forgiveness isn't the same as protecting the perpetrator from natural consequences.

Forgiveness also does not mean forgetting. Jesus forgets, but we don't. Forgiveness built on "forgetfulness" is a Christian version of a frontal lobotomy. Pretending something did not happen does not address the reality of the event and its consequences. Real power comes in remembering *well* without the sting of retribution fantasies.

Along these lines there is a form of forgiveness that on the surface seems sincere but is actually a false substitute. It is a pseudo forgiveness that is premature and glosses over the wound too quickly. This kind of glossing over isn't so much a release from debt as it is the victim's reluctance to face the realities head on. It is a denial that prefers to move on quickly without one feeling the pain of the stark reality. Unfortunately the issue isn't really taken care of and rears its head again in unexpected ways.

Dan and Chrissie had been married for six years, and Dan thought things were going great in the marriage and life in general. He worked hard for his family, and they enjoyed a very comfortable middle-class existence. On a crisp fall day, he picked up the mail and innocently opened the credit card bill, only to discover that the account was maxed out to its very high credit limit. Upon further examination, he discovered that their substantial checking and saving bank accounts were close to being wiped out and that various other household bills hadn't been paid. A heated conversation with Chrissie followed, and she eventually revealed that she had been gambling over a period of months and had gone through all of their credit and cash, which they had designated for buying a house.

Dan, who by nature was meticulous with finances, was furious and threatened to leave the marriage. Chrissie apologized profusely and made an appointment with a counselor to prove her resolve to make positive changes.

After a few days, Dan's anger began to wane, and by the time they arrived at the counseling appointment, he was in a much more positive frame of mind. As the details of Chrissie's betrayal were shared, he appeared to be quite matter-of-fact, with no sign of anger or frustration. When it was time to share his feelings about Chrissie's actions, he shrugged and said, "I've forgiven her. I was really mad at first, but then I realized I needed to forgive her, so I prayed about it and let it go. I'm fine to move on. I'd rather not talk about it. It's no big deal."

While I believe Dan had begun the process of forgiveness, and I commend him for his willingness to let go, it was naïve to believe that the problem was anywhere near resolved. In fact his desire to avoid talking about it was a strong sign that he was avoiding the real impact of Chrissie's problem. He wanted to move on without too much emotional interruption. This is an example of premature forgiveness. It was premature because Dan hadn't yet emotionally experienced the full impact of the consequences. It's like forgiving someone for poking you with a knife, when he has, in fact, cut off your leg.

Forgiveness is most powerful when it acknowledges the depth and extent of the wound and still lets go. Sometimes the details and the impact of the wrong emerge over time, and forgiveness lets go piece by piece as more and more is revealed.

Forgiveness isn't the same as leaving oneself vulnerable to further sinful or cruel behavior. You can forgive and keep your distance if it is likely that further pain will be inflicted.

There are some red flags that indicate that the process of forgiveness is either unfinished or prematurely granted.

- Preoccupation with the one who caused the pain, along with an insatiable desire to understand what went wrong.

- Rehearsing the wrong in your mind, along with possible responses to make the situation right, fair, or just.

- Increased heart rate and emotional response when you're in proximity of the person who hurt you or when you learn of possible proximity to him or her.

- Satisfaction upon hearing about the person's misfortune and thoughts such as, *That serves him right* or *God is paying her back.*

- Over-identification and intense emotional response to similar events in other people's lives.

- Bitterness toward a certain race, gender, or personality type because he or she is like the person who hurt you.

Wait

One of the most difficult things about bouncing back is waiting out the process of recovery. There is no substitute for time—no way around it, no shortcuts. Considering our culture's preoccupation with instantaneous solutions and personal desire for quick relief, it seems terribly inefficient to wait for anything. However, time is a nonnegotiable component of recovery from trauma and pain.

I'm not very good at waiting. It's not part of my DNA. Quite the opposite, my goal in life seems to be finding quicker ways of getting things done. When our son was four years old, he eloquently pointed this out to me. I was getting ready to run errands with Arden in tow. Before setting out down the road, I coached him on how we could more quickly get out of the car and accomplish our tasks in the most efficient way. Eyes wide open and attentive to my instructions, he remarked, "Mom, we're a fast family, aren't we?" I'm fairly certain my epitaph will read, LET'S GET THIS SHOW ON THE ROAD.

The upside is that I get things done—job accomplished, box checked; let's move on. The downside? Well, there are many! Among them are making careless errors (as most of my grade school teachers noted on my report cards), missing emerging opportunities and making hasty judgments which come back to bite me because they are incorrect. And so I'm forced to wrestle with this tendency to hurry and intentionally seek more rest in the face of urgency and impatience.

If we let it, our faith can add a component of urgency. As believers we are drawn to the miraculous deliverance offered in the Scriptures, and we often pursue it with fervor and determination. No one wants to stay in a difficult, painful place. As discussed earlier in the book, seeking relief from pain is well ingrained from the very beginning of our lives.

It is vastly comforting to discover that the Scriptures offer plenty of examples of God's power to intervene miraculously. We have come to believe that God delivers, providing heavenly interference and dramatic turnarounds as he wills. After all, Abraham, Moses, Jonah, Samson, and even Paul experienced miraculous, instantaneous intervention.

But wait... Abraham waited one hundred years for a child; Moses spent forty years in the middle of nowhere (even before the whole Pharaoh and plagues thing); Jonah sat in the stomach of a whale for days; Samson sat blind in prison; Paul wrote much of our treasured biblical books as he sat rotting in jail.

Apparently waiting is a necessary part of life. When we are in the moment of distress, however, this makes no sense at all. What is God up to? What kind of a father would stand by, stroking his chin, simply observing a child in obvious distress? To be honest I've pictured God that way a time or two. The image brings feelings of frustration and anger. I internally protest, *For heaven's sake, God, Do something!*

One challenge to waiting patiently is our finiteness. Forced to exist within the framework of time, we live in the here and now, experiencing sensations—both good and bad—moment by moment. In the moment, pain is unwelcome and abhorrent. Therefore we urgently seek deliverance. *I was fine yesterday,* we may think. *Today there is pain. Pain is bad. I want to be fine again. God, do something!*

God is not finite. He certainly understands time, because he created the sun, moon, and stars, but he does not assign himself to the same structure. He sees the whole picture at once—where I am now, where I am going, and what I need in order to get there. *My experiences today are part of the overall picture and purpose of my life.* Recognizing the greater purpose during a personal season of trial can be monumentally taxing. However, if we embrace the trial with trust in a loving Creator, it gives us strength to continue on. Perhaps the light of full understanding will be dim at first, but trust in someone greater than ourselves will invite us onward.

Waiting appears to be essential to our development. In the moment we myopically cannot see what good possibly could come from our agony, but hindsight brings clarity along with new revelations.

I remember times of distress in my life where I pleaded, commanded, cajoled, and gave ultimatums to God, trying to strong-arm his deliverance. Met with utter silence from above, I fought despair and bitterness and questions about God's existence. Like a fish flopping on the deck of a boat, my ambivalence became a last-ditch effort to threaten God into action. Still he waited.

Apparently I'm a slow learner, but eventually I relented

and considered my options. Quickly I realized I had none—at least none that were viable. In complete exhaustion I surrendered. I put aside everything I knew: all intellectualism, all biblical insight and revelation, all previous experiences. I clung to two things alone—God is God, and he loves me. That was it. And in that moment—miraculously—seeds began to sprout—seeds of peace, freedom, and hope.

I had so much to learn about myself and my own massive contribution to my problems. This required supernatural clarification about myself, but my own resistance stood in the way. God couldn't deliver me until I recognized some things. Ironically I stood in the way of my own deliverance.

If God miraculously had removed me from some of those situations, as I'd desperately longed for, I would have learned nothing. In the moment I was utterly convinced of the solution—others in my life needed to change dramatically. But in the end, it was change in myself that was necessary.

Humans are prone to this kind of dramatic God manipulation. Totally convinced that we need deliverance from our physical affliction or relational trauma, we try to dictate God's agenda in emphatic ways. Because he is grace filled, he is known as one who miraculously intervenes and delivers. However, there are other times when he gloriously and lovingly ignores our insistence and forwards his own agenda intentionally and unswervingly.

Timing

As I've said, my timing is pretty much in the here and now—at least I would prefer it that way. I ask, and God answers. It should be kind of like a vending machine that quickly dispenses a treat when a dollar is inserted.

God isn't like that, however. I once heard someone say with irony, "God is never late. Yet it seems he's just as averse to being early." It's disappointing when God is late by our clock, but it serves us well to remember that God is not a magic genie serving our desires as though we are the master. If he is God, then he is God. We serve him and not the other way around.

There's a colossal human struggle with control and the desire to be the master of our own fates—which is fine, unless you decide that you have made God Lord of your life. The two cannot coexist.

By definition submitting to the Lordship of God leaves no room for the deity of self to assert itself continually and to direct circumstances.

Living in a democratic society (for the most part) makes this idea somewhat difficult to grasp. Picture a kingdom where there is a powerful Lord who holds complete control over people's life and breath. The words "no" and "Lord" in the same sentence would be incomprehensible.

Meaning

Resilience is closely connected with the ability to find meaning in our experience. When it comes to our being able to bounce back, this is probably the last piece that falls into place.

If you try to define meaning prematurely, you likely will be unable to find clarity and grow discouraged. Try to tell a young mother who has only hours ago lost her baby that there is some greater purpose to what occurred. She likely will slap you or run away screaming—and I would have to agree with her; doing so would be cold and heartless. If she's committed to coming back strong, however, she eventually will be able to extract meaning from the tragedy after time has passed.

I never will forget a heart-wrenching visit with a couple that attends our church shortly after their baby tragically and inexplicably died during delivery. That day the visit was more than pastoral. Carl and Molly were friends we had known for years. In fact, Molly had once worked at the church, and because we shared memories with them, my husband and I felt bonded with them as only church staff can. For many years Molly and Carl had waited patiently for the gift of a child. When the news came that they were expecting, everyone was ecstatic. We celebrated the pregnancy in every way possible, and after nine months, we awaited the happy report of new life.

Instead we got horrible, devastating news. Our hearts were broken with theirs when tragedy struck. There were no words to express the depth of our sorrow, and there were none for a very long time. Assigning meaning at the beginning of the grief journey would have been trite and incomprehensible. For Molly and Carl simply breathing the next breath was the priority during those first few days and months.

However, it has now been more than four years since this devastation. Since then Molly and Carl joyfully have welcomed into their lives a delightful daughter and have a strong network of friends and busy, full lives.

Molly recently spoke to me about the great benefits she gained from a social network that had developed during that fated pregnancy. When she learned she was pregnant after ten years of trying, she joined an online pregnancy group. The moms-to-be were from all over the country and bonded over their common experience of pregnancy. When Molly and Carl's baby died, the bond in the group became particularly strong because of their shared grief. The relationships that normally would have waned after the participants reached full-term had been bonded together by compassion for the suffering of one of their own.

Now, several years later, Molly is positively influencing many of these friends as she walks out her own journey to health and wholeness—and they listen because they have walked through the storm with her and have seen her emerge intact and ready to face life enthusiastically. She has become a leader in this network. You might say that good has come out of tragedy. I can tell from Molly's demeanor that she finds meaning in her leadership and influence. Her raison d'être was hard-won, but it propels her forward even when the memories produce lingering moments of sadness.

Reinvest

In the immediate wake of great loss or tragedy, paralysis can set in. In fact one of the common manifestations of shock is a state of daze, a delayed responsiveness and an inability to act. In the initial moments after a traumatic event, people easily can forget how to spell their name or be unable to recite their address.

Unfortunately this predictable initial paralysis can transform into something more chronic and debilitating unless one makes a choice. In the aftermath of trauma, one must decide to get back in the game and reinvest in life. The process may be slow and gradual, but it must be intentional and focused. "I *will* live again. I *will* take care of myself. I *will* act on my beliefs and my value system. I *will* access my faith and other resources that are available to me in order to propel myself forward." And one breath at a time, one step at a time, one moment at a time, inexplicably it becomes true.

These decisions must be cognitive and determined. Feelings may or may not fall into place. The good news about this kind of determination is that it does not wait for something to happen but instead makes a choice.

There is a great deal to be said about showing up. You may have heard the Woody Allen quote "Eighty percent of success is showing up." Showing up can be as simple as getting out of bed, putting on your trousers one leg at a time, walking out the door of your home, and showing up at work or church or a family event, all the while focusing on the next breath. It's a conscious decision to bypass feelings of dread, reluctance, and paralysis and simply do the next thing.

There is power in showing up time and time again. Eventually, slowly, in time, something happens and healing dawns.

Bouncing Back from Failure

In a discussion of resilience, we can't go too far without exploring what to do about personal failure. It is potentially one of the most difficult things from which to bounce back.

No one likes to fail. Every human being on the planet has failed numerous times yet still cringes when faced with the possibility. Too often embarrassment, self-loathing, and regret pile up in failure's wake to serve a bitter taste that leads to rationalization, excuses, defensiveness, and shame.

Sometimes we manage to keep our failure private, while other times it is publically flaunted, adding humiliation to our list of reasons for avoiding it at all cost.

I have been teaching for a long time. In the early days of

our church ministry, I often taught adult Sunday school classes. Teaching was a delight to me, and I came to believe that it was one of my gifts. In those days I felt fairly confident in my ability to provide a positive experience for those who were in attendance. Because of our regular meetings, I had grown fond of the people in the class and believed a bond of mutual respect and admiration had developed. In short I loved teaching, and I loved my class.

One Sunday, during a study of the Israelites' journey through the wilderness under the leadership of Moses, I decided to share a joke I had heard. The punch line was a stereotypical guilt-evoking statement that a Jewish mother might make to her children. Because it made me laugh and because I wanted to keep the class fun, I decided to share it. It made sense to me because we were studying the Israelites. As I look back, however, it was a naïve decision. Upon hearing it, most of the class chuckled good-naturedly, but not everyone did.

A visiting couple (their first Sunday in the class), rose to their feet and announced that they were not amused and were highly offended by the joke's cultural stereotype. They hastily exited the class and demanded to be reunited with their children (who were in age-appropriate Sunday school classes of their own), so they could leave the church. They clearly stated that they had no intention of returning.

I was horrified by my great, public error in judgment. The

first thought that entered my mind was, *The pastor's wife isn't supposed to drive people away from the church.* The second thought was even more devastating. *Everyone in this class has just watched me make a fool of myself.*

Time was drawn out into slow motion as I feebly raised an index finger to the class and said, "I need just a moment please," before bolting from the class. I chased the couple down the long hallway (they were fast) and begged their forgiveness to no avail. They left in a huff.

There was nothing to do but return and face the class. It was one of the most difficult moments of my life. It felt a bit like I was in one of those nightmares where you end up standing completely naked in front of a crowd.

I knew immediately that I had made an error in judgment. Naïve or not, I should have known better than to share the joke. My embarrassment wasn't so much about the couple (I was regretful to see them go but slightly annoyed by the way they had handled the situation); it was that I had goofed publically—and in front of my friends.

It's ironic that we should feel such great reluctance to let others see our mistakes. Failing is no great surprise to anyone, because everyone experiences it. No one is exempt from the experience. Only Jesus was perfect. Everyone else—not! Why then do we avoid admitting it, resist disclosure, and hide when we've failed?

It comes back to our incessant preoccupation with self.

Our preoccupation makes what concerns us seem so much bigger than anything else. In truth what appears as humiliating and shameful to ourselves is most likely much less so to others. Spending a lot of time worrying what other people think of us is futile. For the most part, people aren't thinking of us nearly as much as we think they are—even after a major faux pas.

Consider that day in the Sunday school class as an example. Tension rippled through the room as the events unfolded, and I'm sure the observers felt mixed feelings about what was happening. However, compared to the amount of pain that I felt at the moment, theirs was minimal. One hour later most of them likely had forgotten about it, and one day later, they undoubtedly had moved on.

Do the members of my class remember the incident? Probably, but it's unlikely that the memory evokes angst in anyone other than myself. I, however, had a choice. I could choose to allow that single incident to humiliate me for days, months, or even years, or I could choose to acknowledge my humanity, learn from it, and lay it aside.

Admitting our failure goes a long way toward overcoming it. Denying, hiding, or pretending only encourages repetition. Simple acknowledgment says, "I did this. I take responsibility. It was a wrong choice."

Tearfully I confessed my failure to the class, and not surprisingly, they embraced me with comfort and acceptance.

Some commented that they actually felt a closer bond with me after the incident than they had felt before.

We can use failure to our benefit if we apply what we have learned. This means we move from "I made a wrong choice" to "I can make a different choice in the future. What can I take away from this experience?" That way learning becomes part of the process. Failure teaches us what doesn't work, thereby narrowing the choices of what will.

From this one experience long ago, I learned some valuable lessons that have stayed with me to this day.

- Humor at someone else's expense is never appropriate.
- You never know who is represented in the people you teach.
- Teaching is a great responsibility. *Never* take it lightly.

Of course you have the choice to learn nothing at all and let your failure inhibit you from moving forward in your life. Blame, rationalization, and defeat will paralyze. I suppose I could have quit teaching or even left the church, hanging my head in shame. What a tragedy that would have been. Ironically that would have been the greatest failure of all.

Remember that failure has nothing to do with your value as a person. The question of your value was settled at the cross and is not dependent on choices.

Separate the choice you made from your personal value.

Either you chose to say or do something you shouldn't have, or you neglected to say or do something you should have. In either case it was the choice that was wrong and not your value. Separating the two requires mental discipline and a strong awareness of God's grace.

If your position and standing before God has been settled once and for all, failure can become a means of reminding you of your complete dependence on the grace of God. It either will push you toward grace or leave you wallowing in defeat. The choice is yours.

Benjamin Franklin said, "I didn't fail the test. I just found one hundred ways to do it wrong."

Remember, the definition of resilience is "the capability of a strained body to recover its size and shape after deformation caused especially by compressive stress" (Merriam-Webster). "Owning it" means doing everything we can to reinforce the process of recovery when obstacles come our way. This requires something of us. It will be painful; there will be many questions; and the process will be slower than we would like it to be, but in the end, what other choice do we have?

6 MAXIMIZE RELATIONSHIPS

I meet a lot of isolated and lonely people—too many in fact. This isn't to say that people are *alone* in the literal sense of the word—quite the opposite. Lonely people may have lives that are busy and filled with ongoing interaction and connection. It's the nature of the connection that's the problem. It's a connection without true knowing. While a mass of information is exchanged and processed, the personal, heartfelt interaction with others lacks meaning or depth.

It is an urban phenomenon—the "harried lonely." Not obvious to the casual observer, the internal isolation of these individuals largely goes unnoticed. Their brave faces meet the world every day, and most of the time they have become quite comfortable in their isolation, believing they have no other options.

At the same time, ironically, our culture is shifting toward a greater emphasis on relationships, connection, and attachment. Along with that shift, a plethora of research is emerging that validates our tremendous need for meaningful connection. Consider the following excerpt from a 2010 *New York Times* article.

Numerous studies have suggested that strong social ties are associated with better health and longevity, but now a sweeping review of the research shows just how important social relationships really are. Researchers from Brigham Young University reviewed 148 studies that tracked the social habits of more than 300,000 people. They found that people who have strong ties to family, friends or co-workers have a 50 percent lower risk of dying over a given period than those with fewer social connections, according to the journal Plos Medicine.

The researchers concluded that having few friends or weak social ties to the community is just as harmful to health as being an alcoholic or smoking nearly a pack of cigarettes a day. Weak social ties are more harmful than not exercising and twice as risky as being obese, the researchers found.[3]

A 2008 *US News & World Report* article also explains why loneliness has negative effects on our health.

Loneliness shows up in measurements of stress hormones, immune function, and cardiovascular function. Lonely adults consume more alcohol and get less exercise than those who

---

[3] Parker-Pope, Tara. "A New Risk Factor: Your Social Life." *The New York Times.* http://well.blogs.nytimes.com/2010/07/28/a-new-risk-factor-your-social-life (accessed March 6, 2013).

are not lonely. Their diet is higher in fat, their sleep is less efficient, and they report more daytime fatigue. Loneliness also disrupts the regulation of cellular processes deep within the body, predisposing us to premature aging.[4]

The strong correlation between meaningful relationships and physical health is unlikely to generate a great deal of surprise. The benefit of strong personal connections seems obvious. A while back I went to breakfast with three friends at a quaint French restaurant. One friend was moving across the country with her family, so the four of us gathered to say our goodbyes. We talked, reminisced, planned future get-togethers, and tried to encourage our hesitant but expectant re-locator. Because a parting of the ways was coming, we talked freely about the bond we felt for one another. I felt warmed and encouraged by our memories and the mutual love we felt. The deep sense of well-being that came from the nurturing connection of friendship lasted the whole day and into the next.

The relationship among the four of us wasn't perfect by any stretch. In fact our bond was seasoned enough to bring a healthy dose of reality about one another's quirks and rough edges. The warmth stemmed from a deep sense of mutual admiration, respect, care, and shared purpose, as we worked

---

[4] Shute, Nancy. "Why Loneliness Is Bad for Your Health." *US News & World Report.* http://health.usnews.com/health-news/family-health/brain-and-behavior/articles/2008/11/12/why-loneliness-is-bad-for-your-health (accessed March 6, 2013).

together on the staff of a church.

For the most part, we all know that we benefit greatly from the support of others as we walk through the ups and downs of life. Being known by another is a powerful positive influence in negotiating the difficult days that life brings. I recall a time when our son was desperately seeking a job in a very difficult economic climate. After several attempts and rejections, he had one promising interview upon which he based his hopes. He waited all weekend to hear whether he got the job. I received his disappointed phone call on Monday morning. He didn't get the job.

Why did he call me? It was quite clear that I couldn't solve the immediate problem for him. At the time he lived a good three thousand miles away, and I had no way of knowing of any alternative possibilities for jobs. No, he didn't call me to solve his problem. He called me tell me about it. Why? Because he knows I care about him and the circumstances of his life. He called because there's power and courage that comes from encouragement, as well as caring from those who love us.

Talk to someone who has lost a loved one or suffered great trauma. We've recently watched and mourned with entire communities who were impacted by mass devastation either at the hand of a deranged individual or through an act of nature. We've watched as communities and even nations rallied together to support one another and bring assistance in whatever way possible. Those directly affected will tell you that the support and presence of a loving community is hugely significant in seeing them through loss and trauma. There is something very powerful about the caring presence of a loving, compassionate friend.

I've learned that the most healing thing in the counseling process is the relationship between the client and the counselor. Relief is not found primarily—as we would like to believe—in the wise words and insights of the therapist. No, it is the power found in the presence of a caring, safe individual that brings healing far and above what is actually said.

Think about when you last spent time with a good friend or a group of friends. Remember how you felt afterward. Assuming it was a positive, healthy environment, you probably felt uplifted, encouraged, and connected—all positive emotions—despite whatever ominous things were lurking in your everyday life.

I've seen this applied in my own life. There have been times when I left my home to meet with a friend shortly after a tense interaction with my husband (OK, an argument), wondering the whole way whether I should cancel because of my negative frame of mind. In the end I left that friendly interaction feeling hugely relieved and encouraged, even though I didn't discuss my home issues. This is the power of connection.

Why then do so many people report that they are lonely and feel isolated? Plenty of studies confirm this reality. Lynn Smith-Lovin, a sociology professor at Duke University, found that one-fourth of Americans state that they have no one "with whom they can discuss their innermost thoughts, worries and woes."[5] This means that in a room of one hundred people, twenty-five would claim to be lonely. This is a high number.

For most of us, our growing isolation is clearly not due to the lack of physical proximity. Geographic isolation is becoming a rarity. Instead we are isolated by our busy schedules, our lack of community, and our belief that others aren't experiencing what we are experiencing.

As we move through the adult seasons of life, greater effort is required to build and maintain social relationships as we become busier and more preoccupied with our families, children, and careers. Adult life, with its business and hyper-scheduling, makes meaningful interaction difficult and requires intentionality that isn't required in high school or college, which have existing social systems.

Intentional relationships require a determination to make the pursuit of healthy connection as important as personal hygiene or anything else we prioritize due to our deep

---

[5] Baldino, Rachel G. "How to Combat the Growing Problem of Loneliness and Social Isolation in Our Lives." SixWise. http://www.sixwise.com/newsletters/06/07/12/how-to-combat-the-growing-problem-of-loneliness-and-social-isolation-in-our-lives.htm (accessed March 6, 2013).

convictions. Time, effort, and risk are all required. Even though we may deeply wish for magical intervention, rarely will it "just happen" because we are in the right place at the right time.

Observe well-connected people, and you'll note that they're willing to invest time and energy into the pursuit and maintenance of their friendships.

If connection doesn't come naturally to you (as evidenced by your lack of meaningful interaction), become a relational learner. Observe, study, learn, and grow. Above all be invested in your own personal growth and maturity. As you advance, the health of your relationships inevitably will advance because the fact remains that relationships can be no more mature than the members participating in it. Address your own level of maturity, and as it grows, you will make better choices and attract different kinds of people.

I often remind people that personal growth tends to change the configuration of one's social network. For example boundary-less people tend to attract people who also are boundary-less, because they match. If one pursues personal growth and begins to set boundaries, the boundary-less friends likely would be offended and quickly become unhappy, meaning they wouldn't be friends for long. However, others who also have good boundaries now would feel more attracted to the boundary setter.

Connecting Well

Erin met Heather at a birthday dinner for a mutual friend. Seated beside each other at the restaurant, they immediately hit it off. Erin loved Heather's jovial personality and quirky sense of humor, while Heather felt drawn to Erin's stable presence and nurturing demeanor. They exchanged contact information, and that night marked the beginning of a mutually satisfying and rewarding friendship.

Although they both had busy schedules, they managed to communicate frequently through texts and quick phone calls over the next few months, quickly building a close friendship. At least weekly they met for coffee or lunch, sharing the details of their lives and encouraging each other. They both expressed gratefulness for this gift of friendship.

After about six months, there came a time when Erin became aware that Heather wasn't as quick to initiate contact; she also wasn't as timely in responding to Erin's communications. Heather was inconsistent in returning texts, and their get-togethers became unpredictable and sporadic.

Reluctant to say anything at first, Erin began to mentally keep track of the communication and who was initiating what. In Erin's mind it became obvious that Heather was withdrawing from her.

Concerned, Erin brought it up at a much-delayed coffee date. Heather acted confused and somewhat defensive, saying she didn't really know what Erin was talking about and that she cared about the friendship as much as she ever had. The conversation left both of them feeling confused and defensive.

At one time or another, every relationship will experience some sort of tension between connection and separateness. Both are necessary in a healthy relationship. Finding the balance between the two is an ongoing dance of self-definition and cooperation.

Self-definition is crucial to health in relationships because it defines the edges of self. That is to say, where one person ends and where the other begins should be an ongoing, honest, mutual exploration. Self-definition compels each person to own his or her preferences honestly and without apology. At the same time, it allows each person to free the other to be himself or herself without the strings of self-validation or personal gain.

If both Heather and Erin were well-defined…

Heather might clearly let Erin know that she periodically needs space in order to regroup, and she would non-defensively clarify that this need isn't a reflection of how she feels about the relationship.

Erin would know that she is a good friend who has a life beyond Heather and is therefore accepting of Heather's need for space at those times, turning instead to other sources of self-care in her life.

Being well-defined does *not* mean that we do precisely

what we want to do with no regard for the other. It means exactly the opposite. When self is well defined, we have nothing to prove and therefore become free to release others to be themselves, even cooperating with them to bring about what they need.

While Erin might miss the frequent contact with Heather, she would be able to give Heather the benefit of the doubt when she withdraws. She also would be confident in herself as a good friend and ready to reengage when Heather is ready.

Heather, on the other hand, would own her desire for periodic space, admitting to it and asking clearly for what she needs during those times. This is the cooperative part of the equation.

Cooperating with others' separateness means allowing the other to be a person with individual needs. Allowing this requires maturity and self-care. Let's say Erin is really looking forward to a scheduled shopping excursion with Heather. She has had a rough week and has comforted herself with the anticipated time with her friend on the weekend. On Saturday morning, Heather sends a text stating that she isn't feeling well and would like to postpone shopping. Erin is very disappointed and now suffers the loss of the anticipated stress-relieving excursion. At this moment she has the choice to either 1) vent her grief on Heather, implying that she's failing as a friend; or 2) express her condolences to Heather and move to plan B for the day.

The second option would require more self-control on Erin's part, as well as greater effort in carrying out an alternative plan. However, it also would bring greater freedom to her friendship with Heather, not to mention a better day for her.

Both Erin and Heather would benefit from reevaluating their approach to friendship and the amount of connection and distance they feel they require. If they're willing, they'll learn something about themselves that will empower them to better negotiate their friendship and future relationships.

Unhealthy connection demands compliance and cooperation from the other in order for the relationship to be OK. Anything else leads to hurt feelings and tension. Healthy separateness allows Heather and Erin to be two individuals with differing needs, each responsible for her own. Heather might offer an alternative time to get together, while Erin might consider what else she could do to meet her need for friendship connection.

Enmeshment

When two people become so attached that they hardly know where one ends and the other begins, they are *enmeshed*. This term, taken from Family Systems Theory, refers to a relationship in which individuality is surrendered to make room for group thinking, acting, and believing. Strength and self-worth are drawn from the relationship bond itself. The bond seems to validate the existence of the participants. This in itself is not a problem until the bond becomes more important than the individuality of the members. In enmeshed relationships, people are over-involved with each other to the point of losing themselves in order to attach strongly. Emotions swing up or down based on the amount of cohesiveness or "alikeness" between the enmeshed parties. Differences are seen as hindrances to the bond and are sources of tension and pain in the relationship. Members quickly learn that agreeing with and validating each other maintains stability. Spouses can become enmeshed, as can parents with their children, and friends with friends.

You may have observed a relationship between two friends who appear to be together 24/7. They seem to come as a package deal. It quickly becomes clear that you wouldn't dream of extending a social invitation to one without inviting the other. You know that anything that is discussed with one will be shared with the other. All other relationships (whether it's marriage or family) take second place to this bonded relationship.

If you could observe the dynamics more closely, you'd see some common characteristics that are present in an enmeshed relationship.

Extremely high expectations for loyalty, affirmation, and validation are present at the expense of individuality.

Both people spend a great deal of time discussing their relationship with one another.

Both people express great affection toward one another that borders on neediness (e.g., "I couldn't live without you").

Tensions frequently develop over perceived slights, inattentiveness, and any hint of rejection.

The most unfortunate tendency of such a relationship is the predominant self-blindness regarding the unhealthy dynamics. Enmeshed participants often vehemently deny what is obvious to observers, insisting instead that the relationship is a healthy model for closeness and mutual care. The relationship so powerfully feeds the ego and the unmet need for validation that its participants feel great resistance toward seeing the downsides.

Detachment

On the opposite side from enmeshment lies detachment. A detached relationship values safe separateness as the primary need. The relationship is superficial and transient. Vulnerability is avoided, usually out of fear of rejection or self-abasement. Social interaction is limited to very controlled, safe topics that do not expose the participants' difficulties or vulnerabilities.

Such relationships seem to run their course within a period of time, with the participants experiencing an increasing, indefinable emotional distance. Over time feelings of attachment gradually fade, leaving the participants feeling apathetic toward the relationship. Having reached that point, neither person can define exactly what happened and therefore come to believe that the withdrawal was inevitable. The detached former confidantes only know that their feelings for the other waned and therefore assume that "it wasn't meant to be."

It isn't uncommon to have couples in such a predicament make one last effort to revive the relationship by exploring couples counseling. In such a case, the first session is rather predictable. The couple will report a lack of passion in the relationship to the point of their having apathetic feelings for each other. They'll describe a relationship dynamic that amounts to parallel living under the same roof. In other words they're living their own independent lives with relative harmony between them. They'll report a largely conflict-free relationship with little to disagree about. Often they'll claim that the other person is their "best friend," adding that while they still love each other, it is a platonic love.

At this point I, as their counselor, am likely to ask them to describe the conflict in their relationship. I suspect what I am about to hear. In most cases they will sincerely and truthfully report that they have none.

Without intending to, a couple like this has, by avoiding conflict, chosen distant safety over open vulnerability. Unfortunately for them, the fact remains that true intimacy isn't possible without conflict. The very statement sounds contradictory, but it's true.

Conflict occurs when differences emerge in such a way that causes tension. The emergence of tension is a fact of life and inevitable in any honest relationship, whether we like it or not. When the couple explores the tensions in non-destructive ways, intimacy grows as more is mutually revealed about each person.

An early but intense conflict in my marriage was precipitated by Werner's good intentions to "help me" by cleaning out our kitchen junk drawer without my consent. We had a long, loud discussion about boundaries, order, and our personal preferences surrounding the situation. We learned (albeit painfully) what we now know about each other—that on a deeper level, the "incident" was fueled by Werner's almost compulsive desire to get rid of clutter (explained by his past) and my obsessive need to have a voice (also explained by my past). Those are very important truths about us that wouldn't be obvious to most observers. Werner and I clearly know these vulnerabilities about each other because of this conflict (and others like it), when we learned a great deal about what makes each other tick. The relationship has grown over thirty-something years of revealing ourselves through honest discussion and conflict.

This is why couples that proudly claim that they never fight are either lying or perhaps truthful but unconsciously avoiding conflict. No one agrees with another person all the time. The degree to which disagreement is avoided is the degree to which true knowing is avoided. Furthermore no one is 100 percent OK with another person all the time. If people try to be, they're being false and insincere and are covering up the real issues.

It takes courage to have conflict, especially when early family conflict was especially painful in a person's life. The prospect of conflict terrifies some people. It is no small thing to be very afraid of conflict, especially when one fears that it will irreparably destroy the relationship, as was modeled in earlier destructive family situations.

Healthy attachment seeks honest connection and interaction with safe people with whom there is freedom to connect in a way that is meaningful to both parties.

In a healthy relationship, each person in the relationship is strongly connected, but needs are expressed and directly take into account the convenience and preference of everyone in the relationship. During times together there is appropriate honesty and vulnerability as well as freedom to respond or not respond as a separate person. Individuals can disagree respectfully or opt out of a discussion if they are not ready to approach the topic. There is freedom from the demand to meet every need, and freedom to feel honest feelings.

Safe relationships are built on the basic underlying understanding that no person is alone responsible for another's well-being, nor is any one person another's last resort. Maturity offers the understanding that while it is appropriate to ask others for help, input, or support, ultimately responsibility rests with us. In other words we *own* our needs.

Faith in a loving, relational God compels us to submit ourselves to his grace and therefore have him become our first and last resort. Other humans in our lives never were meant to carry that burden.

Charles was a single dad with three children under the age of eight. He had the very difficult task of juggling his career, parenting, and home management. Upon learning that Fran, the young neighbor woman, didn't mind caring for his children occasionally, he began to seek her assistance on a regular basis and soon gratefully came to depend on her availability. When an opportunity arose for a business trip that could very well advance his career, he assumed she would be available. Fran, however, shyly declined, saying a family weekend had been planned. A good salesman, Charles launched into an effort to convince Fran to relent. His arguments were very compelling, but the zinger was his assertion that if she didn't do it, his career would be affected. He let her know in no uncertain terms that she was his last resort. Not wanting to be the cause of such devastation in his life, Fran changed her plans. However, it was the beginning of a gradual deepening rift in the relationship.

While it seems that Charles was way off track in his forceful manipulations to get what he needed from Fran, both Charles and Fran had an unhealthy approach to relationships.

Charles believed that a true friend should be obligated to bail him out of trouble over and above her own needs. He was partially wrong about this. The trouble is with the word "obligated." A friend has the opportunity to help but must have the freedom to choose on a case-by-case basis, factoring in other obligations and a life beyond the friendship. As compelling as Charles's need was, he still carried responsibility regarding the outcome of this dilemma. Fran was one possible resort, but she couldn't be the only one. Even though Charles felt he had no other options, this wasn't in fact true. Effort would have been required, and even though it may have been difficult for him to pursue other options, he certainly had them. Owning it would have meant releasing Fran, exploring those options, and reaching out toward other alternatives.

Fran was pulled into this unhealthy interaction by her fear of disapproval from Charles and her fear of possibly losing the friendship. Because of this she wasn't truly free to choose her options, which inevitably led to the distancing between the two of them. There is no true safety in a relationship without the freedom to be a separate person.

When a Relationship Hurts

Being a grown-up in a friendship requires ample doses of both self-denial and self-awareness. It requires self-denial because one must factor in the other's needs, wishes, and preferences. It requires self-awareness because one cannot share what one does not know. Both of these traits are most severely tested when wounds are inflicted. The irony of friendship—or any relationship for that matter—is that, given time, there will be wounding on both sides.

Negotiating these seasons of friendship requires a great deal of maturity and courage. This is further complicated by the fact that everyone involved must choose to work things out in order for rifts to be successfully negotiated.

Without going into conflict-resolution strategies, let's say that chances for reconciliation and repair are much greater if both parties are prepared to keep communicating as maturely and non-destructively as possible.

Seek for and take ownership of personal contributions to the problem; acknowledge them; apologize.

Barring personal danger, be willing to communicate about the issue, taking appropriate breaks *until the issue is resolved.*

Put yourself in the other person's shoes, and make a great effort to see the issue through his or her eyes.

Stretch by seeking solutions that take everyone's needs into account.

Unfortunately we can't get around the fact that sometimes

a rift develops that is irreparable, and the relationship disintegrates. It may not be your choice, but remember that both sides must choose to pursue connection in order for the relationship to continue. When this happens and you're left as the abandoned party, it can be incredibly painful and tap into every abandonment issue you may have.

Recently this reality hit home for me. I attended a social event where I greeted a person who had intentionally and deliberately severed ties with me that were once close and family-like. There was a time not so long ago when a greeting would have inspired laughter, warmth, and self-disclosure. Now, in response to a greeting, there was strain and discomfort. The perfunctory hug felt stiff and uncomfortable, and the mumbled greetings were hurried and obligatory. As I walked away, my heart broke all over again.

Unfortunately, in human interaction, there isn't always a solution that will repair a chasm. Our goal always should be to work toward reconciliation, but there will be times when it isn't possible. Many factors contribute to such a self-protective response.

The injury is too severe, and the broken relationship is a consequence of our own bad choices.

The injured party is a conflict avoider and would no more deal with this conflict than he or she would deal with any other. (This pattern would be pervasive in all of his or her relationships.)

The injured party sincerely believes he or she has done everything possible to communicate his or her feelings, but feeling unheard, has given up.

The uncooperative party is self absorbed and unforgiving.

You may have already learned that there are no magic words that will bring down the walls and initiate repair. This is because, in a relationship, the other person also gets to choose. Once again we must confront the reality that some things are beyond control, and therefore they just hurt.

In the wake of such a breakup, we again must choose between freedom, life, and health, or resentment, pain, and defeat. We must grieve the loss of what we long for, but as we work through that grief, it will be necessary to let go of what we cannot control, while diligently pursuing forgiveness every step of the way.

Triangles

In a group of friends, Amy had a problem with Brea. Amy decided to speak with a mutual friend, Cassie, to help her sort it all out. Cassie, who was well connected with both Brea and Amy, felt very concerned about their rift. In a moment of empathy, she passed her concern along at her book club, which was attended by Gail, another mutual friend. Gail, who happened to good friends with Brea, felt uncomfortable with the information and informed Brea that she had been the topic of conversation at the book club. Brea was very hurt by

Amy's betrayal and brought Gail up to speed on the facts of the conflict with Amy. Gail went back to the book club and reported her conversation with Brea to the interested hearers. Brea, now feeling uncomfortable and unsafe, distanced herself from everyone except Gail, who seemed to be her ally. In time her relationship with Gail became strained as well. All were bewildered and hurt and wondered how things got so complicated.

While the names and details are fictional, this scenario may ring a little too familiar to be comfortable. It wouldn't be much of an exaggeration to say that a similar course of events is played out all too frequently in many of our communities. In the name of sparing the feelings of others, issues are dealt with indirectly and covertly; they simmer below the surface, where they fester and remain unresolved. In the meantime good relationships are undermined, and teams are rendered less effective. Clearly this approach to conflict resolution is inadequate and futile and ultimately creates more chaos than solutions.

If A has a problem with B and approaches C to discuss it, a triangle is formed. If C then approaches another, who turns to yet another, more and more interlocking triangles are added. The more triangles, the more complicated the communication becomes.

In many social networks, triangular communication is a chosen response; on the surface it appears to be the kinder, less invasive approach. When faced with relationship tensions, the third party in the mix invites a seemingly safe solution that offers relief without the pain of honest revelation.

When we engage in triangles, we would like to believe that we are nobly sparing feelings and preventing painful interactions. We tell ourselves that the third party is helpful, offering objectivity, refuge, and solutions without upsetting the fragile state of the relationship. On the surface this sounds admirable. It is, however, a trap.

Below the surface lurks a more sinister motivation. Self-preservation and power grabbing are covered in a cloak of niceness and concern for the other. This is because the third party offers validation and affirmation. We generally deny this kind of self-revelation, but in moments of true honesty, we must admit that our motivation weighs heavier on the self-serving side than what is best for the other or for the relationship.

The most obvious challenge with this triangular communication is that it is indirect. It's a little like trying to sink a golf ball in a hole behind a wall, rather than in a straight-line shot. At the very least, it will take two shots and each shot adds heightened vulnerability to further obstacles and human error. It is in fact worse than that analogy because of the human factor. People simply lack objectivity. When we share our perception of events with another human being, the other person interprets it through a grid of his or her own experiences, projections, values, and worldviews. Your recitation of perceptions and events is filtered through my grid and emerges on the other side diluted and somewhat skewed. Each time it is passed along, it becomes a little more contaminated, much like in the childhood game Telephone. When Amy confided in Cassie, Cassie listened to Amy's concerns and subconsciously added her own assessments, unresolved issues, and preconceptions about Brea. It quickly becomes clear that triangulation is notoriously inefficient, especially in the resolution of conflict, when a great deal of clarity and careful listening is required.

The second negative effect of triangulation is the weakening of the primary relationship (i.e., between Amy and Brea). Essentially it diminishes the bond between the two friends. Several dynamics contribute to the problem.

First, when a third party enters the interaction, it reinforces the pattern of avoidance in the relationship between the original two (Amy and Brea). Because talking to the third party (Cassie) almost certainly will reduce Amy's tension, it will feel like relief and therefore will reinforce Amy's decision to talk to Cassie. She could tell herself that it was the right thing to do and justify doing it again the next time tensions arise. Amy will feel somewhat better after sharing with Cassie, because she has diluted her stress by obtaining validation and concern. Of course very little has been solved, and her relationship with Brea has been undermined, but she'll feel better for a short while.

Unfortunately Amy now has a secret that will become another brick in a wall that is being erected between them. The next time the issue arises (and it will because it never was resolved between them), she will have a little more reason to seek relief in the way that worked before.

The other part of the problem is that Amy and Brea are not practicing direct conflict resolution. Each time people substitute other methods, the direct approach becomes a little less comfortable and a little more intimidating. It also invites further indirect resolution of problems. Amy and Brea will grow further and further apart while likely feeling confused and baffled about it.

Finally, Brea is clearly at a disadvantage in the interaction. She isn't given voice to speak from her perspective. She also is robbed of the opportunity to learn something about herself and about her friend. In the name of being spared, she actually is excluded, minimized, and denied the opportunity to be part of the solution.

The question then might be raised as to whether it is ever appropriate to invite a third party into the resolution of relationship issues. The answer is a resounding, yes, with stipulations. There are situations in which it is clearly impossible to communicate one on one. In cases in which a person refuses to communicate or becomes abusive in language or action, it is necessary to pursue other options. However, it is a last alternative and has drawbacks. The limitations of such an approach must be recognized and acknowledged. If we were to look at the options as a decision grid, it would look something like this.

Option 1: Both parties speak directly one on one, clarifying and validating and offering solutions.

Option 2: Both parties meet in the presence of a third party who seeks objectivity and clarity from both sides.

Option 3: One person in the relationship speaks with a third party alone in order to gain another perspective and wise input. Preferably the third party isn't close to either side and therefore is much more objective. Even so there are limitations to this approach. It is a "make-do" solution, not a best-case scenario.

Passive-Aggressive Behavior

Not long ago I joined a group of married friends who were bonding over a lighthearted and spirited discussion, when the conversation turned to shopping. The avid and somewhat compulsive deal finders in the group compared notes then compared their spouses' reactions to their shopping exploits. Those seated around the table shared stereotypical wife-husband interactions. Lucy proudly said that her husband didn't care what she bought and never questioned her decisions. Mary offered that she and her husband used an envelope system that gave her freedom to spend whatever was in the designated envelope. Sharon rolled her eyes and muttered something about her husband's tight control over the finances. But it was Charlotte who laughed and pulled out a red Sharpie from her purse. "This is my *magic* marker," she sang out. "My husband checks the tags when I come home, so I simply mark everything down with my red pen before I get home and tell him it was on sale. It works great and everybody's happy."

If we're going to discuss taking responsibility for our lives, we have to talk about passive-aggressiveness. Passive-aggressiveness is a conflict-avoidance mechanism that stands in direct contrast to the goal of seeking maturity in relationship. Essentially it is a way of indirectly controlling and manipulating things to get what we really want.

What is passive-aggressive behavior? At the risk of oversimplifying the definition, it occurs when one appears to go along with something outwardly while inwardly resisting. It's letting one's resistance be known in manipulative ways.

For example:

- It is showing up significantly late (or not at all) for a party that you didn't want to attend in the first place.

- It is not being able to "find" that documentation after multiple requests to produce it—because you secretly think the request is unreasonable.

- It is smiling and nodding in agreement despite inward

bells and whistles to the contrary—and then gossiping about it with a mutual friend.

- It is acting as if your feelings aren't hurt when they really are and distancing yourself ever so slightly.

Get the picture? Passive-aggressiveness is the false outward appearance of cooperation, designed to keep the peace while inwardly disagreeing and resisting. It serves two purposes.

- It allows a person to appear cooperative, agreeable, and helpful, thereby serving to build self-value.
- It is an attempt to avoid the consequences of direct disagreement or boundary setting.

In other words it is motivated by 1) pride; or 2) fear. Does this sound harsh? Maybe…

This kind of conflict avoidance, however, causes a great deal of unresolved pain in relationships and has the opposite effect of bringing people together. It builds subtle but palpable walls of tension behind what outwardly appears to be cooperation and regard. Put a bunch of passive-aggressive people in a room, and everyone will smile and make nice, but there's no way of knowing what everyone *really* thinks, as undefined tension rises in the room. There can be no true "knowing," because no one's sharing his or her real self, which is the basis of true intimacy. Over time the agreeable feelings fade, because beneath all of the smiles, conflict, tension, and distance simmer.

In Charlotte's case her behavior was motivated by a few things.

- A desire to buy what she wanted without accountability to her spouse.
- A desire to avoid the negative effect of hearing his protests.
- A desire to look cooperative and accommodating (the good guy) without actually being so.

On an even deeper level, Charlotte was failing to acknowledge her anger toward her husband—anger she successfully had hidden even from herself, masking it under the guise of humor. In truth she was doing her own thing with total disregard for her husband's preferences—a hostile act. She also was robbing him of his right to express how he felt about her choices.

Is it always undesirable to resort to passive-aggressiveness? I've thought about this, and my answer is "yes." While "passiveness" in itself (e.g., not responding, or hiding one's true feelings) may be appropriate, even life-saving at times, it's the "aggressive" part that becomes problematic. That's the part that punishes or pays back in subtle ways (forgetting, distancing, rejecting). It's just not OK. Even though there's a cooperative façade, it's hostile in nature, and it brings about division.

The alternative is congruency. This simply means that what you speak matches what's inside. It risks revealing your true self. It understands that a façade of agreement isn't the basis for depth in a relationship. It does *not* mean that you say whatever enters your mind (that would be *stupidity*); it does mean that what you choose to speak is consistent with who you are. Obviously this can lead to tension at times, even if we graciously seek to minimize the impact.

There are ways to communicate potentially tense messages in a direct way with kindness and grace. Fortunately it is a skill that can be practiced. For example you might say:

- I'm sorry. I know it's very important to you, but I won't be able to make it.

- Since you asked, I'd have to say I don't completely agree with you, although I respect your perspective.

- I love spending time with you. However, I've never been a fan of _____ (insert activity). Would you mind if we did something else?

- I want you to know that I value our friendship, but I did feel hurt when you _____ (insert action). Can we talk about it?

These are expressions of self. They speak what is inside. At moments like this, tension is unavoidable. However, dealing with differences directly is the only way to resolve issues in a way that honors the relationship in the long run. Think of it this way—risking short-term tension can lead to long-term depth of the relationship.

I guess it depends on what you want. If you just want absence of conflict in the moment, I suppose passive-aggressiveness will serve you well. You'll avoid a moment of tension by saying what you think someone else wants to hear. In the long run, however, you'll sacrifice the depth of the relationship because you won't be able to really expose what you think. In the end there will be a different kind of tension in the relationship, won't there?

Try congruency instead of passive-aggressiveness. Take a deep breath. Take a risk. Speak out. And when you do, celebrate your courage. It's freeing.

So we need one another. This truth isn't big news to anyone. Finding one another and keeping one another seems to be the more difficult piece of the challenge. In this area, as in all the others we have discussed, we are once again confronted with our personal responsibility to take ownership of our needs. Healthy relationships are unquestionably the stuff through which life becomes meaningful and tolerable. We cannot afford to be lax about our pursuit of mature connection.

Doing so requires tenacity, courage, and commitment despite obstacles, but then almost all good things in life require the same.

"If you haven't found it yet, keep looking. Don't settle. As with all matters of the heart, you'll know when you find it. And, like any great relationship, it just gets better and better as the years roll on."

—*Steve Jobs*

CONCLUSION

After completing the paperwork, Flora settled back in her chair and struggled to find the words to bring voice to the difficult circumstances that had brought her to her current place of quiet desperation. Tears appeared in her eyes before she could utter the first word. She apologized profusely for crying. "I didn't think I was going to," she said. With difficulty she discussed the recent events in her life that had contributed to her current state of grief, hopelessness, and confusion.

As she did, her story began to unfold. I listened carefully and asked a question here and there to help unpack the details. My job in those initial moments is to listen well and to seek to understand how the various pieces of a client's narrative come together and weave the tapestry that is his or her experience. This process is one of the most compelling parts of my job—the piecing together of a person's story. It's not only the story itself but also the experiencing of it, the feelings, the perspective, and the interpretation of it. Most often, in the sharing, pieces of insight begin to fall into place like big puzzle pieces that snap into place on a grid.

"I think my marriage is ending after twenty years and three children. I never saw it coming." *Snap.*

"My parents are divorced." *Snap.*

"My older brother has ADD, and my parents spent a good deal of time trying to figure out how to manage his gigantic presence in the home." *Snap.*

"I was my maternal grandmother's favorite and spent a great deal of time at her home." *Snap.*

"By nature I'm compliant and shy. From childhood I kept to myself and never made waves." *Snap.*

"In my marriage I always went along with everything. Everything was basically his way, and I let it be so for the sake of peace." *Snap.*

"After staying home with the children for ten years, I recently went back to work." *Snap.*

"I'm well liked at my job, and the company is promoting me." *Snap.*

Piece by piece a story emerges. The narrative includes family history, personality leanings, genetics, uncontrollable circumstances, personal choices, biology, and spirituality, among other things. The details of Flora's story made her unique and special.

At her current crossroads, Flora had the choice to own her story or to brush it aside in the interest of quickly feeling better. Brushing it aside would mean finding relief for her pain as quickly as possible. Feeling better would be the goal. Getting into a new relationship or medicating herself in some way could quickly accomplish that. Trust me—human beings are remarkably adept at finding ways to self-medicate.

"Owning it" would mean taking a good hard look at her current situation in the context of her whole life, thereby gaining new insights and depth of learning that are only possible in hindsight. It would then mean intentionally moving forward after having learned something. If Flora was like most people, she would not consciously choose, but a decision would be made nonetheless.

At the beginning of this book, we asked ourselves, "How do we find authentic meaning in life without exhausting and discouraging ourselves in the pursuit of it?"

We have learned that reaching this goal has something to do with embracing the gift of life itself. It has everything to do with making peace with the bits and pieces that encompass the entire journey of living and then using what we have learned to more wisely propel us forward.

Grow Up

Physical maturity happens quite naturally and predictably. On the other hand, achieving emotional and relational maturity requires a concerted and intentional resolve.

Become Aware

We cannot change what we do not know about ourselves. Self-awareness is a knowledge we can cultivate and nurture, much like a muscle we strengthen.

Define Values

We are compelled by our values—*always*. There's no way around it. Rather than try harder, take a hard look at your priorities and honestly admit if you think they are out of alignment.

Take Responsibility

This is the crux of maturity. Break past your own resistance and acknowledge your role in every circumstance. In our current culture, incidents of 100-percent victimization are rare indeed.

Cultivate Resilience

Resilience is the ability to bounce back into shape after being stretched. It requires internal cooperation and a willingness to emotionally process events in a way that extracts meaning from all of your life experiences.

Maximize Relationships

Healthy relationships comprise a large part of a healthy, fulfilled life. At the same time, they require effort, unselfishness, and a willingness to risk being vulnerable. Cultivating strong relationships also requires a conscious pursuit despite the obstacles and inconvenience.

Life is waiting to be lived to its fullest. It requires from us a willingness to be a part of the process and to embrace and examine our lives in ways that bring freedom, understanding, and competence. No matter your age, you're in for a lifelong process that is never quite completed or wrapped up.

Maybe you've encountered those tragic souls who never got past the difficult fragments of their life story. It's tragic because it is quickly evident that they are stuck and have failed to move forward with their lives. In their "stuckness" they have become entrenched in their own impotence and have relinquished the contributions they could make to the world.

On the other hand, we all have encountered people who have used every experience, every blessing, and every challenge to extract something from life that will make a maximum positive impact. These individuals make more of a difference every day in life because they have owned life.

Which will you be?

"If you are not happy with your life, you can change it in two ways: either improve the conditions in which you live, or improve your inner spiritual state. The first is not always possible, but the second is."
—*Leo Tolstoy*

APPENDIX

The following is list of relationship rules for grown-ups. People frequently ask me what it means to be a grown-up in relationships. I developed this list as a quick-reference tool that outlines the basic concepts of mature connection.

Adult Relationship Manifesto

1. I understand that no one has it all together. I don't pretend to be perfect, nor do I demand perfection from others.

2. Realizing this, I'm open for feedback and strive to overcome defensiveness in order to wisely assimilate what I am hearing.

3. When I make a mistake, I admit it, do what I can to repair the situation, and move on, wiser for the experience.

4. I ask for what I want in appropriate ways, realizing I won't always get what I want from others. I recognize that ultimately I must own my needs and come up with alternative solutions when others are not able to help me.

5. I recognize that friendship and trust grow over time. I do what I can to invest in the relationship in positive ways. I invite reciprocation without demanding or coercing others to give me allegiance and trust.

6. I recognize that not all relationships will work. A relationship takes two willing people who have time, energy, and the desire to invest. Sometimes circumstances outside of my control will make it impossible for a relationship to go in the direction I would like it to go.

7. I take responsibility for my life and my circumstances and refrain from blaming others for my problems.

8. I'm committed to self-growth no matter how painful it may be. I'm aware of the human tendency to have personal blind spots. Therefore I will carefully and prayerfully examine my own life and progress over time.

9. I'm aware of the human great need for connection. I'm

also aware that our current culture doesn't necessarily promote an environment in which relationships are easily formed and strengthened. I'll therefore be proactive about seeking and building positive, healthy connection with others in my life.

10. I'll strive for congruency in the way I communicate with others, meaning I will align my outward expression with my inward thoughts. This doesn't mean that I express every internal inclination. It simply means that when I choose to communicate, it matches what I feel and believe.

11. I'll expect others to be congruent as well, allowing them to assume responsibility for whether or not they speak truthfully. I'll take people at face value and expect them to speak up for themselves and communicate what they need.

12. I'll relate to others as an equal adult, not lording over them with unsolicited advice and direction, not being inferior and needy, and not putting up with unwanted and destructive interactions.

13. I'll keep my word to the best of my ability, being honest in the first place about what I truly believe I can deliver

and communicating clearly my inability to follow through in those cases when I can't deliver for reasons that are beyond me.

14. I'll respect others' right to space and privacy. This means I respect others' right to choose something other than what I'm proposing, and I won't take personally decisions to choose alternatives to engaging with me at any given time.

15. I expect to be treated courteously and honorably. When I'm not treated in a respectful way, I'll take steps in my power to protect myself from harm, firmly communicating my disagreement and then taking steps to remove myself.

ACKNOWLEDGMENTS

How do I begin to acknowledge all the people who have helped me, encouraged me, urged me onward, and challenged me (in a good way) with regard to this project? If I begin to name them, I'll surely leave someone out. The point is that I'm blessed with a plethora of wonderful people in my life who stand ready to love, encourage, and support me whenever they can. You know who you are, and I'm forever grateful.

My extended family, where there is mutual love and the sure knowledge that we all would drop anything and come rushing to one another's assistance if anyone needed anything. Our heritage brings a firm foundation of common sense, a strong work ethic, and resolute determination, for which I'm so grateful. We live way too far apart, and I miss you all constantly.

My Oregonian, Texan, Canadian, and German church

families, who have loved and encouraged me for more than thirty years.

My counseling colleagues, who have kept me sharp and taught me new ways of approaching life (even though I've secretly wondered whether everyone else is much more knowledgeable than I am).

My clients, who have taught me that patience and timing is everything and that unconditional regard is much more powerful than eloquent words.

My friends. You know who you are. I think I've been blessed more than the average person to have multiple relationships with girlfriends who are real, honest and life giving. Many issues that we have discussed and processed over coffee are woven into the pages of this book. I could not do life without you. Your words of encouragement came just at the right time and kept me going countless times during this project. I'm eternally grateful.

My editor, Katie Naylor, who nudged me to better writing, offered great alternative ways of saying stuff, and constantly cheered me on. I always will be thankful that just at the right time we reconnected after all those years.

Finally I'd like to thank my husband Werner and our children, Alison and Zach Piepmeyer and Arden Rienas. Werner, you have been my greatest cheerleader every step of the way. I am blessed to partner with you. You make the journey fun. Kids, you guys are amazing. We've been a real family with ups and downs, great times, and hard seasons. The hard times have challenged us to dig deeper and to grow up faster. During the good times, we celebrated one another and the joy of being together. We've laughed a lot and enjoyed one another's uniqueness to the fullest. My greatest joy is seeing you all thrive. Thank you for standing behind me and putting up with a wife and mom who has analyzed you more than once.

ABOUT THE AUTHOR
GABRIELE RIENAS, MA, LPC

Gabriele is a Licensed Professional Counselor (LPC) in Oregon and has been in private practice for more than twenty years. She has worked with individuals, couples, and families regarding a variety of life issues. She is known for her practical, insightful approach to life and her ability to communicate complex truths in a humorous, down-to-earth fashion.

As the wife of a minister for the last thirty-five years, she has extensive experience in community life, including working with volunteers, training leaders, planning events, and raising funds. Her passion for sharing principles of practical living is expressed in classes, conferences, counseling and everyday conversations.

Often invited to teach in both community settings and churches, she weaves her experiences - both positive and negative - into her teaching and writing. Topics include Healthy Living, Overcoming Trauma, Relationships and

Marriage, Parenting, Leadership Principles and Intentional Living.

Gabi travels nationally and internationally, speaking at women's events, marriage conferences, and leadership training forums. She also consults organizations on relational and behavioral issues.

She is a contributing columnist for *Enrichment Journal*, a magazine that focuses on faith-based leadership issues. For the past eight years, she has addressed the practical concerns of ministers' wives.

Gabi and her husband Werner have two children—Alison (who is married to Zach Piepmeyer) and Arden.

To contact Gabriele visit www.gabrielerienas.com.